In difficult times, challenges and change

BE YOUR OWN ROCK

THE PROVEN WAY TO STRENGTHEN
YOUR MIND AND BUILD THE
POWER TO OVERCOME ANYTHING

SAGAR CONSTANTIN

Be Your Own Rock
The proven way to strengthen your mind and build the power to overcome anything.

A book from Constantin Publishing House

SagarConstantin.com

ISBN: 9789694392240

Special thanks you to my editor Henriette Bohnstedt and to my amazing proofreader: Janell Parque http://janellparque.blogspot.com

Download the workbook and more free resources from sagarconstantin.com/byor

CONTENTS

Introduction   vii

Learn to master changes, challenges, and difficult
times, no matter how hard it seems.   1

PART I
1. The Requisite for Succeeding with Change   17

PART II
2. Change Is the Most Certain Thing in Life.   25
3. Change—an Opportunity or a Curse?   28
4. Step out of the Comfort Zone   33
5. The Unconscious Fear of Change   39
6. Meet Amygdala – the Brain's Guard Dog   47

PART III
7. What Creates Your Identity?   55
8. The Foundation of Your Identity   63

PART IV
9. Creating a Buffer Zone   75
10. Understand Your Brain, Understand Yourself   77
11. The Limbic System   85
12. Becoming Emotionally Intelligent   90
13. Neocortex   95
14. Make it Easy—Make it Attractive   109

PART V
15. The Root Cause of Reactions   119
16. Know Your Survival Strategy   141

PART VI
17. Is Change a (Hate) Gift?   149
18. Are You in Control?   155
19. The Three Levels of Change   162

20. Resistance to Change   171
21. Shift Focus!   174
22. Stages of Change   179
23. Know your ABC's of Psychology   190
24. Setting Healthy Boundaries   197

PART VII

25. What Is Your Inner Strategy?   207
26. Doer—Fast and Decisive   214
27. Thinker—Structure and Perspective   222
28. Feeler—Intuitive and Empathetic   232
29. Changer—Flexible and Ready for Change   240
30. Getting to Know Your Personality Type   251
31. Overview of the Personality Types' Response to
    Change.   254
32. Understanding Your Inner Balance   263

PART VIII

33. Understanding Yourself and Others Yields the Best
    Results   269
34. Do You Want To Be Ready for Change?   273
35. Learn from Life   276
36. Be Your Own Rock   279
37. MAPPED   282

Recommend the book   285
About the Author   287
Get in touch   288
More books by Sagar Constantin   290

INTRODUCTION

Everything is alive, everything is connected, and everything changes.

LEARN TO MASTER CHANGES, CHALLENGES, AND DIFFICULT TIMES, NO MATTER HOW HARD IT SEEMS.

Changes are everywhere, and they will not stop or slow down. The world is moving faster than ever before. It doesn't matter where in the world you are; the intensity of changes has increased: Wars, natural disasters, diseases, and inflation. We are all feeling it. No one knows how the future will look or what tomorrow will bring. But you can get ahead, be comfortable, and succeed with changes no matter where they occur in your life.

It doesn't matter if it's at home or work; you must deal with changes daily! You have already met many changes and have most likely been challenged by changes, too—especially those you didn't have any control over. Maybe you are fed up with changes, but know you can't control when and what changes hit you. They come when you least expect them and often when you don't want them. Looking back at the significant changes in your life, you will see that you have learned a lot. But many people quickly forget and move on to the next thing in their lives. Often, we miss out on great learning opportunities and insights from changes and challenges because we are eager to move on or are too afraid to face the real cause and take the needed steps.

To succeed in life, we need to be able to deal with changes and challenges; otherwise, they will tackle us, define our destiny, and leave us behind, or, even worse, we will become negative and give up. Changes are the most certain thing in life, but they also challenge us the most. At the same time, we get bored if nothing changes.

In my work delivering business lectures, I meet many leaders who are poor at managing changes. Honestly, they are a disaster. After a lecture with a shipping company, one of the leaders looked at me and said, "Sagar, we have done everything wrong. I'm so embarrassed. Everything you say we shouldn't do is what we have done. I have been so blind." I told him it is impossible to do anything different until you become aware. And it's always possible to share your new insight with others and let them know that you did your best, but now you can do even better.

In the ancient wisdom of Tao, they believe that everything is energy, and the flow of life consists of three pillars: Everything is alive, everything is connected, and everything changes.

When *everything is alive*, it also means that everything will pass eventually. Life goes on; it doesn't stop just because of a change. The soul's journey is long, and the Taoists see everything as living energy: nature, humans, furniture, buildings, and light. And when everything is alive, it is also able to change.

Everything is connected. We are all dependent on each other. When a tsunami hits one shore, it can affect many other countries and people all over the world. Not just the people living nearby but also their relatives, friends, and people who have heard about the disaster are impacted. When one country neglects the importance of looking after our planet, it affects people and nature worldwide. It's like rings in a pond. You throw a stone, and the strongest effect is at the center. But it will cause a ripple effect. A war in one country causes prices to go up in another country. When Tesla dropped the prices of the Model 3 and Y in 2023, it caused a ripple effect on the whole industry. And when a cargo ship gets stuck or attacked, it will cause shortages elsewhere.

Everything changes. When we are in the middle of a change, it can be hard to see and discover what we are learning from the change. Instead, we are caught in the fight and struggle. But this, too, will pass. Tomorrow will be different if you let it and know how to work with the flow of the change instead of fighting it. Change is the most certain thing in life. Nature changes, seasons change, and we change. Just imagine for a second that we didn't. Imagine you got stuck when you turned 21 and had to keep your interests, hobbies, way of life, education, and awareness level for the rest of your life. I'm sure you would find it boring and unsatisfying after a while. There are so many changes every single day that we don't notice or take for granted. And then there are the changes we fight against. We don't want to look older, but nature dictates that our body ages. We don't want to let go of our kids, but they grow up and want to live their own lives. We love our job, but there is a reduction in sales, and people are fired. Everything changes....

In this book, I will give you the key to succeeding with changes, challenges, and difficult times. I will share the things that will make your approach to changes shift forever. I will enlighten you about the deep forces in all human beings regarding changes and how you can take back control of your own life. Learning the simple tools in this book will help you feel calm and rooted in yourself when you deal with changes in the future. You will be able to succeed with changes in your life that you have failed with so many times before.

You will learn to deal with changes and challenges that include:

- Career and Financial
- Health and Well-being
- Relationship
- Motivation
- Ability to succeed with your dreams
- Changes and challenges brought upon you

I will teach you how to change your habits, lose those extra pounds, or make changes at work. Even more important, I will reveal the deepest secret, explaining why we resist change and give up before reaching our goals.

By the end of this book, you will never again wonder what it takes to succeed with a change or miss out on learning from it. You will be able to deal with a change without feeling stressed, having your thoughts run wild, or becoming nervous.

With the insights in the pages ahead, you will be able to understand your reaction to changes and how changes influence other people. You will not only thrive with the changes you experience, but you will also be able to help and support others.

"Changes are a constant factor; it is how we react to them and learn from them that defines us."
    -SC

Hannah Got Rid of her Arthritis

In 2019, I held a lecture at a company where Hannah is employed. The lecture included two of my favorite subjects: *change* and *personal growth*. In my opinion, those subjects can't be separated if you want to succeed with changes. A few hours into the lecture, Hannah shared with me that she was suffering from arthritis, and it was so painful that her doctor said that she would probably have to resign from work in a couple of years. She was upset because she loved her job and enjoyed being with her colleagues. But the pain in her body was overwhelming. She had tried all kinds of medicine, but the side effects were so devastating that she preferred the pain. She was fifty-two, and she still wanted so many things in life. She wanted to travel, enjoy being with her grandchildren, and start playing pickleball with her friends. None of it would be possible now, and her pain and ability to move would only get worse. Then, she said one thing that caught my attention. "I know what can ease my pain, but I don't do it. And I'm so angry with myself. Why don't I have enough backbone or willpower to do what is needed to get a better life? How much pain do I have to feel before I make the changes in my lifestyle that are needed?" The answer to that is simple.

"Most people don't make a change in their life until the fear of change is less than their pain."
-SC

Let's delve into that for a second. This is the essence of why change is so hard for most people. The fear of change needs to be less than your pain. When Hannah finds it hard to make the necessary lifestyle changes to feel better, it is not a matter of time, resources, or talent. Her fear of not getting better if she makes the changes prevents her from doing it. What if it doesn't work? Then she would know for sure that she had to live with the pain, and all hope would disappear. So, she sticks with the pain, even though she is unhappy and afraid.

Most of us have a lot of unconscious fear that stops us from making the changes that would benefit us. The fear of succeeding is one that many entrepreneurs have; the fear of failure is one many people know of—why bother? I will probably fail anyway. Then, it's better to brag about how you could have been a superstar if you went for it. But you never did. You wasted your talent because of unconscious fear. I will let you in on other aspects of fear later in the book so you can learn how to deal with it in a healthy and constructive way that can benefit you. In the lecture I taught where Hannah attended, I shared insights I will share with you in the book—insights that changed Hannah's life forever.

Hannah didn't say much for the rest of the day, and I didn't think much about our talk afterward. Fast-forward to two years after the lecture and the Covid lockdown. I was giving a new lecture at the same company, and a woman approached me before we began. "Do you remember me?" she started. I shook my head; I didn't recognize her. "I was in your lecture two years ago, and you taught me how to make a change that would last."

"Oh," I replied. "That's great."

"You still don't remember me, do you?" I shook my head again. "I'm the one suffering from arthritis... but I look different now. I lost 20 kilos." My jaw dropped, and I remembered right away.

"But..." I stammered, and she just laughed and continued.

"Because of what you taught me, I went home and made a plan, just like you said, and I stuck to it. Today, I can work, and I hardly feel any pain. The arthritis is at a low level, and it's not a problem. So I can enjoy my life and have a future. I'm so grateful for your insight and tools; they changed my life. I just wanted to let you know." I was speechless. It's one thing to teach tools and insight, but when I meet people who take responsibility and use it all to make a significant change in their lives, I am blown away and deeply grateful.

My Search for a Better Way

I know what it's like to make significant changes in your life and how intense the fear of change can be. In my life, I have learned to become friends with fear, so it doesn't prevent me from doing what is best for me. I have undergone two significant career changes and have been divorced twice. My first career change occurred when I was employed at Channel 2 in Denmark as a director (Channel 2 is one of the national television stations in Denmark). I started at the TV station as a trainee and advanced to the position of director. With a promising career ahead of me, I decided to resign and start my own business. Was I afraid? You bet. I was thirty years old and had a great career in front of me and all my friends at the TV station. My entire life was about working at the TV station. My identity was Channel 2. My manager once said I was the greatest talent in the television business he had ever seen, and the CEO told me I would be his successor. Why would I give up all of that? Because the pain I was in grew more significant than my fear of a change. Behind the scenes in the sports department, there was jealousy of my position. Another director who had been there much longer than me started to make my life a living hell. She lied and manipulated me in a way I didn't realize until years later. She turned out to be a psychopath, and I had never dealt with anyone like that before. I was naïve and trusted her like I trusted everyone in my life. In less than four months, my life turned upside down. People I thought were my close friends stabbed me in the back, and from being a sought-after person, I became the center of gossip. Only one person came to me and asked if any of the rumors were true since she didn't believe a person could change that fast or have fooled so many. At that moment, I realized what a bad situation I was in. And I asked myself if I believed I could make it all go away and return to what it was before. Even though the answer tore me apart, I knew it to be true. I had to leave. I wrote a farewell email to all the employees so they knew that I was sad to go but had no choice and that I had had the best time and would miss most of them.

At that point in my life, I didn't have the tools or insight to deal with a change of this magnitude. I continued my life and survived the best I could. Before resigning, I had called a former colleague at the other national TV station, Channel 1, and signed a one-year contract. I knew I had to leave the television business, but I wasn't ready yet. One year gave me time to work out what I wanted and prepare for it. At least, that was what I thought and what kept the change manageable. There was a huge cultural difference between the TV stations, so it was difficult for me since I was brought up at Channel 2, the younger and more vibrant station. Channel 1 was old and dusty. The change was hard, and I never settled in. But it gave me time to find my grounding again and have a time out. Then something unexpected happened. When the year was nearly over, I met a man through mutual friends who told me about *feng shui*. At first, I thought it was funny and a little bit strange. My upbringing wasn't spiritual or religious, and I knew nothing about personal growth or Eastern philosophies and practices. But I was curious and attended a lecture he gave a week later. That was mind-blowing for me. I felt like the blinders had been removed from my eyes, and I could see a deeper meaning of life. This was what I was going to do. I was ready to leave the television business behind. Not long after, we became a couple and rented a place together. We decided to establish a conference center in our apartment. We told family and friends to pass on the message that we were offering courses in what we called *"neo-feng shui,"* a new way of using *feng shui* where interior design was combined with personal growth. Since I didn't know much about any of it, I did all the marketing (which at that time wasn't much since social media didn't exist). We were so naive. No one attended our courses, and we failed. I was tempted to go back and get a job in television, something I knew I was good at and the easiest way to make money. But a voice deep inside me kept whispering that it was not the way to go. I wanted to begin living, not just surviving. We didn't make any money at all, and my savings were nearly gone. I remember that moment like it was yesterday. We looked each other in the eyes and said, we are broke and went to play a game of tennis. I felt a huge sense of calmness and freedom, and at the same time, I kept telling myself that my fallback strategy could always be television. This was my chance to begin from scratch and ask myself what I really wanted to do if I wasn't driven by fear, ambition, or the need to be recognized. We decided to move from Copenhagen back to Aarhus (the second largest city in Denmark, where I was born and where my mum and dad still lived). We only had the deposit from our apartment but were lucky to get more than our deposit back since so many people wanted our place and offered us money for the lease. We had no other income. We rented a place to live in Aarhus but couldn't let go of our dream to teach *neo-feng shui* and make it into a famous brand. After we settled in, we decided to try again. This time, we were more prepared and found a three-year lease in the city and created a conference space. This was a bold move since we still didn't know if we could sell any seats at our courses. And at this time, I had no experience giving lectures and only knew little about the wisdom. But we succeeded! It became a huge business in the next five years, and we made millions. We worked with some of Denmark's most famous hotels and large companies and had a long waiting list for our courses, which private people attended. I wrote a bestseller about *neo-feng shui* that was translated into five languages, trained several hundred consultants, and gave lectures to over 10,000 people. Since then, changes and life lessons have just been lining up in my life. After five years, we divorced, and I sold my share of the company, not knowing what to do next. A few months later, I began to write a novel (*The Life*). It took me six months and inspired me to begin to teach insights from the book. At the same time, I was trained as a psychotherapist and developed an educational program for personal growth. After some years, I shifted my focus to giving lectures to companies, and I am now the highest-rated lecturer at the biggest course provider in Denmark. I got married and divorced twice in the next ten years and had two amazing boys. I have lived in twenty-five different places in Denmark since I moved out from home at the age of 16, and I have also lived in Australia three times and in London. I have learned to love changes the hard way and always challenged myself to choose what felt right rather than take the easy way. My curiosity has led me into all kinds of situations, and at times, it has been so difficult that I nearly lost hope things would improve. But they always have. No matter how tough it's been, I have come through stronger, happier, and wiser.

Today, I have been giving lectures for over 24 years and have written eight books. Thousands of people like Hannah have experienced changes that have defined the rest of their lives.

Succeeding with Change

When I meet people and companies that are failing with changes, it is because they are not aware of the drivers in the human brain. Leaders don't understand why employees are not excited about the changes.

In our private lives, we believe people who say it is a matter of willpower, or we buy an expensive coaching program, where stories about others who have succeeded in losing 20 pounds provide hope that it will be us one day. But we struggle and fall back into old patterns. It's easy to be fascinated by other people's results and successes. I do it as well. But I always remind myself that they are not showing us the whole truth. It is a business. A BUSINESS. They are selling something using psychological triggers. A dream. A hope. And sometimes quick fixes. And as long as you hope your life will change, you are unhappy, or have low self-esteem, they can sell you anything. There are no quick fixes. But it doesn't need to be complicated, either. I think the most important thing is to get started and be patient— whether you want changes in your life or to be better at dealing with the changes that are brought on you. When you change your approach to life, you will learn and progress daily. You will know that you will never finish. I will give you the tools and wisdom to achieve lifelong success with any change in your life. You can stumble on your way and have to get up again, but you can't fail. That's it.

The tools I'm going to share with you I also teach in my lectures. The most frequent feedback I get is how amazed people are to discover how easy it is to implement in their lives. I'm always hired by companies, but people use the insights both at work and at home. Here is what Søren from LEGO wrote on LinkedIn after I held two lectures for his department.

"In navigating the complex waters of organizational change, I've found an indispensable resource in Sagar Constantin's course 'Smart About Change.' It stands as a beacon for leaders and teams facing significant transitions. Its compelling blend of personal wisdom, scientific insights about the brain, and practical tools has piqued my curiosity and provided a shared language and strategies beneficial for our collective journey."

"Having led teams for over 20 years, I've encountered numerous methodologies and guides, but 'Smart About Change' is the first to elicit universally positive feedback from my entire team. Its impact is evident in how we've incorporated the learnings into our daily operations. The credit goes to Constantin's exceptional ability to be present, communicate effectively, and meet individuals where they are. For any leader or team poised at the brink of change, seeking both understanding and actionable guidance, I wholeheartedly recommend 'Smart About Change.'"

—Søren Hougaard, Senior Manager, LEGO®

PART I

The Fundamentals
Why lasting change is not a quick fix

1

THE REQUISITE FOR SUCCEEDING WITH CHANGE

In my intense studies for the past twenty-four years into human psychology, change, and behavior, I have found that some essential factors are needed to make a lasting change. Many people set out to make a change in their lives repeatedly but fall back into old patterns or give up before succeeding. The top three areas where most people want a change in their lives are career and financial change, health and well-being, and relationships. And I find that health is an area where many people are especially struggling. When I ask my students what they tried to change, they usually answer: lose weight, exercise more, and eat healthier. If there was one easy thing you needed to do or a pill you could take to succeed, there is no doubt many people would. We love when things are easy and no effort is needed. If you want to lose weight, there is a prescription that has become extremely popular. People who have never succeeded in losing weight are now triumphing. However, not everyone can get a prescription to help them; there are side effects to consider, and it is not the solution for everyone. Neither medicine nor technology will save us. Medicine might make us look younger, but we're not, and technology can't replace wisdom or emotions. Emotions are the human driver for personal growth. When you want a change to happen, you need emotions. You can have gadgets, daily planners, and all good intentions, but if you are not aware of the underlying forces in the human brain, none of this will do you any good. You will still be riding the waves, feeling the rush for a while, and then swimming exhausted to shore, waiting for the next wave to ride.

Let me ask you this: how many times have you set out to make a change and failed? One, five, ten? More than twenty? Have you lost count or given up and are telling yourself you won't succeed with the change anyway, so you might as well just let go and eat what you crave? Or are you making excuses? Does it have to do with your upbringing or DNA? You don't have what it takes? Or perhaps you don't have the time or money to get the proper help? The amazing thing about humans is that we are so alike. It doesn't matter where in the world we live. Our brain is wired the same way, and in my studies, I have been amazed to find so many answers to why we behave as we do. Knowing this gives you a choice to continue as you have always done or make a real change. It's your choice—a choice you can make right now and begin to change in the direction you want. Are you game for it? Let's go!

MAPPED!

As a lecturer, psychotherapist, and business coach, I have helped thousands of people make lasting changes and deal with changes brought onto them from the outside. I have MAPPED what I found to be the most important steps to follow when you want to make a lasting and positive change. And when you work with these simple steps and insights, you will be able to make lasting changes in your life. How long does it take to make a lasting change? I get that question all the time. Some people tell me that they heard it takes twenty-one days to change a habit, or some say it takes three months. And I always tell them there is no answer that fits everyone. It depends on the change, how long you have been doing what you want to change, and how much fear and time you have. It depends on you. So, if anyone tells you that you can change in a certain amount of time, it might not be true; many circumstances influence a change. And just because I can do it, it doesn't mean you have the same prerequisites to do it. But you can learn. Hold on to that.

These are the pillars for a lasting change.

Meaning

There is no change without a purpose. If you don't know *why* you are making the change and don't have a positive feeling about it, you will fail. It's that simple. Your emotions will either make you give up or hold on. Our emotions are the inner driver, and they will activate excuses or resistance if you are not happy with the change and convince you to let go or fight the change. Positive emotions will help you succeed with the change and hold onto your new path.

Awareness

We are all different and have various ways of dealing with change, so awareness is crucial—awareness of yourself and others. Being aware of your emotions and reactions is essential when dealing with change. Awareness allows you to observe how your emotions influence your thoughts and actions. Our emotions, whether acknowledged or not, are the inner drivers that will either support or resist change. Without awareness, you may unconsciously fight against the very change you need. But when you are aware of your emotional state, you can better navigate your circumstances, making it easier to move forward.

Plan

Be specific when making a change. It is not enough to say I want to lose weight. How many pounds? And how will you do it? What will you eat? When and where will you go shopping? What will you do if you are going out? Planning is crucial for getting started and sticking to the path. The plan should be so specific that you know exactly which steps to take and when, and it must be easy to follow.

Persistence

We are impatient and don't have time to wait for the results, so we move on to something else or let go of our intention. We live in a world where the pace is getting faster and faster, but it doesn't align with the laws of nature. You can't improve your condition just because you went running once or lose a pound because you quit sugar for one day. We must dig deeper, find the real motivation to make changes and be persistent.

Effort

Make it easy and make it attractive. Use your resources in the best way possible. If I were to give you one piece of advice on change, this would be it. This is where most people fail. We are unrealistic about our ability to stick to our goals and the effort needed to achieve our dreams. We aim way too high and then give up. We struggle instead of enjoying ourselves. The changes we strive for are too hard to accomplish, so we fall back into our old pattern.

Dialogue

Be honest. Be appreciative. Listen. Again and again, we fool ourselves. We are convinced that we are motivated for or want a change, but deep down, we don't. When we listen to our inner voice and emotions, we become much wiser and capable of dealing with changes. It is not a lack of skills or knowledge that prevents us from succeeding; it is our inner dialogue.

Dealing with Changes

The changes we decide ourselves are one thing; however, it's another thing to deal with changes brought upon us. These are two different entities—both can be hard when you don't know how to approach them or don't have the necessary tools, support, or awareness. It's usually much easier to deal with the changes you decide for yourself. You are prepared and have spent time thinking it over. And you are motivated (hopefully). When nature, your manager, or your partner decides on a change that affects you, it can come as a surprise and knock you over. These changes are often underestimated in terms of the inner challenge. We try to deal with these changes with our common sense and logic and fail. We try to fight the changes and lose. I'm sure you will learn with the proper training if there is a new IT system at work. If your partner wants a divorce, you will move on and, in time, find someone even better to share your life with. And if nature causes a disaster and leaves you without a home, you will survive. It will be hard, and your life has taken a sharp turn, but you are alive. As human beings, we are programmed for survival. Our brain has one primary focus, and that is to survive. So, we will manage, but emotions will attack us and make the change difficult.

I always welcome changes and stay curious about what they have to offer me. A new opportunity? Learning? A new connection? When I was younger, I tried to plan as much as possible and always be ahead of the situation. However, I was forced out of my comfort zone and had a pull inside that made me challenge myself constantly. Many changes have marked my life, teaching me to live optimally and manage change. I hope this book will help you understand and work with the changes you make in your life or changes that are brought upon you. The best way to get the most out of the book is to practice the small things and make lasting progress. Do the exercises in the book and download the workbook and more free resources from sagarconstantin.com/byor. That will help you stay on track. Be aware of your own and other people's reactions; that way, you will be the master of changes in your life.

Let's get started,

PART II

Understanding Changes and Challenges
Let's be friends instead of enemies.

2

CHANGE IS THE MOST CERTAIN
THING IN LIFE.

The seasons change, and we grow older. Change is a natural part of our lifecycle, something we all live with. We react only when changes occur unexpectedly or affect our sense of security. There's a significant variance in how well-equipped we are to handle change. Even though, outwardly, it may seem like we can easily manage change, it doesn't necessarily mean that it feels easy for us.

The way we handle change often depends on our inner state. If we are in a good place emotionally and are in balance, we manage it more easily. However, if we're tired and somewhat stressed at work or in our personal lives, a change can seem overwhelming, especially if it comes at an inconvenient time.

All individuals have different predispositions for handling change. Children who have experienced multiple school changes can either learn to be resilient, or the opposite, early in life. Strategies may have been acquired to cope with these changes. Losing good friends and security and being the new student can be incredibly demanding and challenging. Initially, these strategies will act purely for survival, allowing the child to navigate new situations, even if they may feel shy, vulnerable, and uncertain.

With the numerous changes comes a sense of familiarity for the child, experiencing their capability to handle these changes. If the child, as an adult, becomes aware of their history, they can use this ability to manage changes positively. However, if they are not conscious of it, their reaction might lead to a desire to control their life and seek security and predictability, both at work and in their personal life. This way, as an adult, the individual avoids situations that resemble the insecurity and instability experienced during childhood.

Children of divorce also learn to handle changes, both positive and negative. They must navigate between two families with different rules and living conditions. If there are tensions between the parents, they must learn to manage or de-escalate conflict, even though it should be the adult's responsibility. At an early age, they can learn that it's possible to adapt and have their fundamental needs for love and security met, even though they live in two different places.

There is no doubt that, fundamentally, humans are adaptable to change—it's deeply ingrained in us and is part of our survival strategy. However, many people are spared from significant changes throughout their lives, and when they do occur, they can seem overwhelming. Consequently, encountering changes or making choices that bring about changes can make us uncertain about ourselves and our worth. Ultimately, changes can shake the foundation of our being, making us feel that our existence is at stake. Therefore, it's important to learn to live with and manage big and small changes appropriately. Changes will sometimes affect your life in a way you cannot control, which is why we get stressed about changes and feel resistant. They can bring about so much discomfort that it requires a high level of willpower and a safe environment to examine the emotions changes bring to the surface. Interestingly, we can train ourselves to approach changes more open-mindedly if we understand the mechanisms and needs at play.

I believe everyone can learn to handle changes, but it requires introspection and acknowledging what is happening inside us. Strategies are good to have, but they can be challenging to follow if our emotions take over and we don't understand the underlying impact of the changes.

Only when we look inward can we start to evolve, accept change, and get the most out of it instead of fighting against it.

3

CHANGE—AN OPPORTUNITY OR A CURSE?

There is a significant difference in whether we view changes as opportunities or as unnecessary evils that disrupt our daily lives. Most changes require us to relate to them, but many are also minor things that we quickly integrate, becoming a natural part of everyday life without significant effort or fluctuations. What seems like a small bump on the road to you can be a roadblock for others. Never underestimate the power of a change.

Your attitude to changes determines how they are experienced and what you gain from them. If you anticipate that any kind of change will be a hassle and interfere with your work or life, then it's almost certain that you will experience it that way. However, if you approach changes with openness and curiosity, considering how you can take responsibility and exert influence, the changes will more likely enrich you and your work. I'm not saying it's always possible to be open and curious. But be aware of your thoughts and emotions; don't throw unbalanced emotions or negativity at others just because you cannot contain them and take responsibility. In that way, you won't say something you wish you could take back or do something you will later regret.

It's not possible to decide to appreciate changes solely through the power of thought. Emotions are deeply rooted in your body and will influence your thoughts, even if you try to act positively and be open to change. Let's say your favorite place to shop for groceries closes. You know there is another grocery shop down the road and try to focus on that. But you feel sad because you have gone to the same shop your whole life and you know the staff and your way around. Even as a kid, you went to this shop. So many memories are connected to the place, and you don't like the people who own the other shop. On the practical side, they offer the same selection of groceries and have an even wider range of organic food that you prefer to buy. So, what is the big deal? Your *EMOTIONS*. You *like* the old place and have fond memories connected to it. The new place is unfamiliar, and you have negative thoughts attached to it. You can't just force positive thoughts around the new place without also finding positive emotions. It won't work. Emotions will keep pulling you back, and you begin to look for things you don't like in the new place—small things like they are out of tomatoes; the old place was never short of anything. Or you can't find what you are looking for; you knew exactly where to find what you needed at the old place.

If you resist change, your negative emotions will affect you and cloud your vision. Therefore, it's necessary to examine your emotions if you wish to change your perspective and attitude toward change. Relying solely on the power of thought is not sufficient.

When I worked at Channel 2, layoffs were announced. Even though I felt pretty confident that I wouldn't be affected, I could still sense a hint of fear. I tried to observe how others at the station handled the uncertainty. Some panicked, but others remained icy calm, pretending it didn't concern them. But it affected all of us, whether we acknowledged it or not. After the layoffs were announced, it took four days for people to be informed. All employees were asked to remain contactable, and those to be laid off would be notified directly. That morning, the building felt like a mortuary. The atmosphere was subdued, and the long central aisle that ran through the whole building was colorless. Regardless of the outcome, I decided to look forward and make the most of it. I felt I had put in the effort that I could in my work, and if that wasn't enough, then I needed to move on. I confronted my fear, and a calmness settled over my body at that moment. I was no longer afraid of the process or the outcome. I didn't get fired. However, the experience certainly taught me that no matter how well I perform, I am not in control of how long I remain at a workplace or who my colleagues are.

If you work as a manager, you often have to communicate changes that come from higher-ups in the system, and even if you might not agree with these changes, you still need to implement them. You must be loyal upwards so you don't convey to your employees that you disagree with the new initiatives. In the long run, this would create a loyalty issue toward management and make the implementation of the new initiatives much more challenging. But you must also be loyal to yourself and your team. So, never sell a change and try to be positive about it if you're not. Be honest about how you feel and pay respect to the decision and management. You can say, "I know this comes at a bad time, but we need to work out how to deal with it." Or "I can understand if you are frustrated; it's not the best timing, but let's see how we can make it work."

Remember, other people pick up on not only what you say but also your actions and body language. So, start by looking at yourself in relation to the changes—your own position and reaction and what you might be triggered by regarding the new initiatives. If you're aware of this, you will be able to remain grounded when presenting the initiatives to others. Be conscious of the advantages and disadvantages of the changes and pay attention to the emotions that might occur when you present the change. This applies both if you present a change at work or home.

Changes at home can also be hard. But here, it is very important to separate those you're in charge of and those you're not. Moving is always a significant change in our lives and very energy-consuming. It takes time to pack, move, and then unpack. But it also takes time to feel comfortable and safe in your new surroundings. And when you move, it often results in many changes simultaneously. Pay attention to how you feel and give yourself time to adjust to the new surroundings. In our minds, a move can be practical, but it dramatically impacts our sense of feeling safe and secure.

If your partner tells you they want a divorce, and you didn't see it coming, you will be in shock. The most natural reaction is to pretend it's not real and think they will change their mind. When you realize the decision is real, you become angry. Later in this book, I will teach you about the different steps we go through in a change so you can see where you might get stuck or need to be aware in the future. But for now, I will stay focused on the emotion since it is the first awareness step to deal with changes in a better way. A change like this can easily be turned into a battle—but if the decision is made and your partner has found another, why fight the change? We fight because of emotions—feeling abandoned, alone, not good enough, and sad. And they are all important and real. Emotions should not be shut off or neglected but dealt with properly. You might see the change as a curse—you love your partner, enjoy your life, and don't want a change. Right now, you have to decide: Do you fight or surrender? If you fight, be aware not to lose yourself. If you surrender, make sure to transform all your emotions, and don't let anything hang unresolved. Use the change as an opportunity to create an even better life for yourself, and make sure to take time to discover what truly makes you happy.

Exercise:

Name the emotions you have felt about a change that has happened in the last six months.

How did you manage the emotions? Did you embrace and accept them or try to shut them down?

4

STEP OUT OF THE COMFORT ZONE

If you do what you've always done, you'll get the results you've always gotten. It can be challenging to break out of habits and the comfort associated with routine. Most people like to be in control and have a surplus of mental resources in what they do. It takes at least six months to feel comfortable when we begin a new job. We must learn new systems, names, and passcodes and find out where the best coffee is and where to park the car. Nothing is routine initially, and our brain works hard to regain control. However, habits and complacency can prevent us from realizing our full potential. We can be bored at work but stay because we can't be bothered finding another job or stay in an unhealthy relationship because we convince ourselves it is better to be with someone rather than be alone. We will miss out on an opportunity for personal growth but also come to a standstill in our lives.

It's essential to challenge yourself and step outside your comfort zone every now and again; if you don't, it will be much harder to do so the day you are forced to. The brain has a system where we learn new things and deal with things we experienced before—everything from new habits, changes, challenges, or working with new people. This system is important to activate every day because it will shrink if we don't. And if it does, it will be even harder to deal with changes and challenges. To keep this part of the brain active and accessible, we must continue learning new things all our lives.

When LEGO's former CEO Jørgen Vig Knudstorp resigned, he said, "The most important thing I can pass on to my successor is to make a lot of mistakes. You only learn from your mistakes, and you have to experiment and dare to take risks. It's about not just following the safe path because then the development stops."

And he is right. I sometimes work with financial departments. And they are not known for being creative. Well, they shouldn't be creative, I guess. When you do the same work repeatedly and don't challenge yourself to learn new things at home, your ability to make changes decreases. Many people working in finance have a more challenging time when significant changes are presented. They resist change and would prefer to do as they have always done. I meet people who do the accounts in a binder instead of using a computer program. And it's not because they are lazy or have decided they don't want change; it is easier to do things the way you know. We are all like that; we prefer to do things our way. Even if there is a better or more innovative way, we will try to hold on to our way for as long as possible.

You can keep this vital part of your brain in shape by learning new things your whole life. It doesn't have to be big and time-consuming things; starting by brushing your teeth with the other hand, finding a new hobby, or just taking a different route to work will help you. If we make the safe and predictable choice every time, we won't be challenged and expand our knowledge and experience.

Another aspect of leaving the comfort zone is the risk of making mistakes. Many people hate making mistakes and work very hard to prevent them. I meet people who are over-prepared at meetings and never get to share their insights because they don't have the whole picture or are afraid of getting a question they won't be able to answer. A woman in a lecture could relate to that, and I asked her what she feared. She looked down and waited a minute before answering. Then she said, "I fear my colleagues will think I'm not not worthy of my position." She paused before continuing. "I know where it comes from. As a child, I always had to fight for my right to be seen. I had four siblings, and I found out if I was the perfect child, I would get my father's attention."

"Are you mostly working with men?" I asked, knowing the answer, but I wanted her to see the bigger picture. She nodded. She was employed at a big company with many male engineers, and her position included both leading and making presentations to the board. She wasn't an engineer but was very good at her job. "Are you only referring to men?" I asked.

She shook her head and smiled, "There is one woman; she always has my back."

We could all hear the pieces fall into place inside of her. We had another lecture two weeks later and agreed that she would try to observe her need for control and see if she could let go a little. When we met again, I asked all the participants to share what they had learned, but hers greatly impacted us. She had challenged herself and attended a meeting where she only prepared what was an absolute minimum. She was so scared to fall through and be outed by her colleagues. But to her surprise, she was more present at the meeting and managed to listen to what the others said instead of solely focusing on her agenda. She managed to be more active, share her take on the matter discussed, and even ask questions. She laughed, "I felt I was cheating at first, but now I can see how letting go of control makes me a better me."

When we were renovating our home, the builders were about to incorrectly put up a new type of gypsum board. I had read the manual to ensure it was done correctly since I hate it when you need to live with a shoddy job or redo the whole thing yourself. I told the builder he was putting it up wrong according to the manual, and he answered that it was how he had always done it. But I'm sorry—that doesn't make it right. And that is the problem with the human brain. It just loves to do things as it has always done. It cuts corners if you are not aware. And it doesn't do what is best for you or others unless you pay attention and force it to set the bar higher. For the builder, there were other things at stake, too. He had made a mistake, and that is often connected to the emotion of being ashamed. On top of that, if he admitted that he made a mistake, he would have to redo it all and tell his boss that he worked overtime to fix it. Emotions are strong motivators for our decisions, no matter if they are good or bad. We often try to cover up poor decisions or even pretend that we didn't know so that we don't feel wrong or inadequate and are not confronted with our emotions, leaving us vulnerable.

If we allow mistakes to be accepted, we will learn more, become more confident, and get better results. That counts for us and our kids, too. Learning from mistakes is what develops our brains the most, and taking responsibility for learning from mistakes is an excellent resource for us and the people around us. In a hospital, a research group tested how a zero tolerance of errors affected the nurses. For six months, they watched two teams. One team was told that they were not allowed to make mistakes. If they did, the manager would get furious, and they already feared him. The other team was told that mistakes were welcome but expected to be fixed and learned from. After six months, they looked at the teams' performances. It turned out that the team run by fear with a zero-mistake tolerance, had made severe mistakes but tried to cover them up. A patient died, and they didn't help each other or share knowledge. Two members of the team had also resigned. In the other team, the situation was quite different. They had made several mistakes but also improved their routines and cooperation. They were happy and trusted each other. Mistakes are one of the best ways to force the brain to learn new things and remain fit.

We may not discover our full potential if we stay in our comfort zone. But it is easier not to risk anything new and stay with what you know. When you step out of your comfort zone, you not only risk making mistakes, but you also risk failure and becoming vulnerable. Even though we know it would do us good to try out something new, the fear can hold us back—the fear of failing, not being able to live up to others expectations, that you are not as skilled as you told others or the fear of others reactions. The fear can be so overwhelming that we can convince ourselves that it's better to stay with what we know—whether it's a job, partner, house, or skill.

Exercise:

- Describe your comfort zone. What do you need to feel secure and perform optimally in your life?

- What would it take for you to dare to step out of your comfort zone?
- How do you feel about making mistakes?
- Have you made a mistake lately and tried to cover it up? If so, what thoughts and emotions made you do that?
- What can you learn from the mistake?

5

THE UNCONSCIOUS FEAR OF CHANGE

Emotions and change are closely linked. Fear, especially, is often the root of resistance to change. However, they are not always understood to be connected; therefore, reactions to changes can be misunderstood. I often see people only focusing on the practical side of the change and never diving deeper into the source of the resistance. If we don't, it will be very hard to deal with the change, and it can bring a domino effect of more emotions and make it even harder to work out what it is all about. I see people being upset about a change at work, and when I ask what is wrong with the change or what is happening, they never complain about the actual change. They tell me that communication has been poor. They feel insecure and are afraid of not getting the training they need. They don't feel included, or they don't know what their role will be. They are *not* complaining about the change. The mistakes many people make with changes are failing to prepare well enough, poor communication, and a lack of interest in other people's emotions. This applies both at home and at work.

The basic things most people fear are:

- Not being good enough
- Losing something or oneself
- Failing
- Being overlooked
- Being rejected
- Not belonging
- Being made a fool of
- Being ridiculed

Fear is an emotion that lies very deep in our nervous system and unconsciously guides many of our decisions. The unconscious fear is most interesting to address when we want to make changes or struggle with difficulties.

When our decisions are fear-based, they are not optimal or well-considered. They are made because we want to avoid or achieve something—not based on what would be best in that situation.

In one of my lectures, a team leader ordered all his team members back to the office. He didn't want them working from home anymore. They were frustrated and upset. They had had three days at the office every week and two days working from home. It gave them the flexibility to make the home situation work better and still do their job. When I asked the leader why he made this decision, he said it would be better this way. But I challenged him and asked for whom? I also asked why he wanted this change since it looked to me as if the team was doing their job and were happy. Slowly, he began to realize that his unconscious fear had made the decision. He was new in the role as a leader and unsure if the team members worked as they should from home. He felt a loss of control, and it was his need, not theirs. He decided to talk to his team and was open to returning to the old agreement. When the fear is unconscious, we need to bring it to the surface where we can face the fear. Unconscious fear lies in the darkness where we can't see it, but we definitely feel it.

Fear lies deep and latent in all human beings. It is associated with basic survival and activates the reptilian brain, which, among other things, controls the impulse to fight, flee, or freeze. This means that when fear sets in, we use the least developed and most primitive part of the brain to make decisions.

Fear is not unconditionally bad; it helps us survive in situations where we feel threatened. It's when fear takes over in situations where it's not productive or controls us in an undesirable way that we need to pay attention.

Unconscious fear can also be hard to deal with since it is unconscious. It takes time and interest in personal development to bring the hidden layers of our personality to light. Sometimes, it can be helpful to talk to others about the changes that challenge you and, in that way, see if it can help to reveal hidden fears. Our unconscious is like darkness. When our fear is in the unconscious, it controls our emotions, thoughts and behaviour. - and it's nearly impossible to do anything about it, since we are not aware that it is the case. It's hard to see anything and navigate when it's dark. When you bring light, it's easier to see the impact of previous experiences and emotions. The light comes when you begin to face the fear for example by talking to someone else and fall through the layers of your personality. Unconscious fear is the most powerful driver in humans, and when dealing with change, it is crucial that you challenge yourself when you feel resistance and see if you can find the unconscious fear that controls you. When you become aware of the fear, it loses its power, and in time, you can let go of the inner fight and embrace the change or accept the challenge you are facing. If you don't face the fear, it will grow bigger, spread to other areas of your life, and slowly interfere with your decisions and your quality of life.

The opposite of fear is trust. If you notice that you become fearful in situations of change, imagine a conversation with yourself in which you ask: "How would *trust* respond in this situation?" or "How would *fear* respond?" That way, you can discover the difference between a fear-based or trust-based answer, and you'll have the choice between the two options. Choosing trust makes your decision more balanced and long-term. If you choose fear, you act more to deal with the situation in the short term. It is perfectly fine to choose fear if you do it consciously. It is the unconscious fear decisions that often challenge us and we regret.

You can choose trust when you feel safe and secure deep inside. You trust that your relationship will be intact, you trust that you will be able to manage a task, you trust that you will get the help needed or the training if there is something you need to learn. You trust that I will let you know if I'm upset with you. You can trust that the people in power will do the right thing, and you can trust authorities. When you choose to trust, you believe that we will help each other and that our bond is strong enough to handle a conflict. Trusting in yourself means that you rely on yourself, and the choices you make feel authentic to you.

After renovating our house, we decided to build a large shed. I asked a friend who used to work as a builder if he would help us. Since it was a rather large shed and a time-consuming job, he asked to be paid for it, which was fair. After we completed the framework, there was some leftover wood. Our house has a fireplace, and the wood would be useful in the winter. But my friend caught me off-guard and said, "Maybe I can take the leftover wood for my fireplace. That would be great in the winter." I was speechless. He knew we had a fireplace. But many years ago, he was in a motorbike accident that had damaged his brain and his short-term memory. Maybe he had forgotten. I had to stop and observe my thoughts and fears at that moment. The top level of my consciousness was, why should I give him the wood? I'm paying him to help. When I dug deeper, my fear told me that if I said no, maybe he wouldn't help us complete the shed. And I knew it would be hard to do on our own. I turned to my trust, and it said: You have been friends for over thirty years; he will understand if you tell him you want the wood yourself. I took a deep breath. Now, I could make a conscious choice. I faced my fear and my trust. Which should I choose? I chose fear. I wasn't ready to risk not completing the shed or him getting upset. And I didn't feel like pointing out that his memory was damaged. Our friendship was more important to me than the wood, and if it would make him happy to get some wood, I was okay with it. When I was aware of my choice, I was totally fine with choosing fear, and I didn't hold it against him. I feel good about my choice, which is the big difference between conscious and unconscious fear. If I didn't look at my fear and just said yes to him, I would most likely be upset or hold it against him the next time he asked me for something. I would carry it with me in my unconsciousness, and it could slowly destroy our friendship. I wouldn't know why I didn't feel like seeing him again. I could also have projected it on the shed and complained about things that weren't perfect, and since I paid him to help, I was allowed to complain.

Just becoming aware of how much fear governs can be pivotal. Therefore, it's important to be curious about yourself and look for situations where you react, either fear-based or trust-based. This way, you'll become more conscious of your reaction patterns and thus be able to respond more appropriately in each situation rather than being controlled by your fear. We have a choice in every moment. Do you choose trust or fear?

It can be difficult to correctly perceive what is being said if you feel fear in the situation. Therefore, it's easy to misunderstand it or react inappropriately. Security is a prerequisite for the message about change to be heard and perceived correctly.

In 2006, my former partner and I decided to sell our summer cottage. It was too expensive, and we didn't use it after we moved in together. Within a few months, the market dropped due to the worldwide financial crisis. I suggested renting the cottage out, but my partner was sure we could sell it and make a good profit. Over time, it ended up costing us a lot of money, and we had two mortgages. We tried to lower the price, but nothing happened. Finally, after two years, a buyer came along. They made an offer that meant losing $30,000. There was just one problem: it had snowed, which made the roof inspection impossible, so they weren't sure they would buy the house. I was so fed up with this house that I suggested that we shovel the snow down from the roof. It was a nearly flat roof, and it should be possible. We went there, got up on the roof, and began removing all the snow. The snow was heavy, and the roof was not that great to walk on. I stopped. What would happen after we got rid of the snow? Would they be able to do the inspection? What about the ice in the downspout? I tossed the shovel down on the ground and said to my partner, "I'm not doing this. If they want the house, they will also want it in two weeks when the snow has melted." I took a deep breath and felt the fear tickling inside of me but also the relief of choosing trust. Two weeks later, the real estate agent emailed the contract. And an hour later, they called. A new couple wanted the house, too, and they would pay the price we asked, so we wouldn't lose any money. Did we want to go with them? Of course, we did, and I'm so happy that I dared to trust.

If you identify yourself with your fear, you won't perceive things in a nuanced manner. Only when you manage to step out of the identification with fear can you see the whole picture with multiple perspectives and nuances of reality. It's like stepping back and getting the bigger picture. When you are identified with your fear, you stand too close and can only see one truth. It can be hard to tell the difference in the beginning and also be aware of the deeper layers, but when you begin to look and ask yourself: How does fear respond? How does trust respond? And is there anything underneath? You will slowly begin to see and feel the difference, and then you get the most powerful choice in your life: Fear or trust.

Exercise:

Identify your fear:

1. What is the specific situation?
2. What makes you react to what is happening or being said?
3. Ask yourself: How will fear respond to the situation?
4. Ask yourself: How will trust respond to the situation?
5. Are there any deeper layers?

6. What's the worst that can happen when choosing fear? And trust?

7. What will you do if your fear "decides?" What will you do if your trust "decides?"

6

MEET AMYGDALA – THE BRAIN'S GUARD DOG

The brain has a function named the Amygdala, which developed to help us avoid and survive dangerous situations. It's created during the fetus stage and works as soon as the child is born. The amygdala records any situation it finds dangerous and saves it, even though you cannot remember it and are unaware of the danger. The Amygdala will hijack your brain if it detects a threat and shut down any unnecessary functions to help you be present and alert in the situation. It activates body reactions like rapid heartbeat, increased blood pressure, and attention. The amygdala is positioned over the brainstem at the bottom of the Limbic system. It is the size of an almond, from which it also got its name: Amygdala means almond tree in Latin.

When we experience a change that we are uncomfortable with or challenged by, the Amygdala is likely to hijack our limbic system. The limbic system is the part of the brain that controls our emotions, among other things. When this happens, it magnifies our emotions; if you are upset, you will be angry. If you are sad, you will be devastated; if you are afraid, you will be terrified. You won't be able to use common sense and consider your reaction, and if asked later why you reacted this way, you won't know. In the moment, you are identified with your emotion, and your whole worldview goes through that emotion. It is the truth to you. When the amygdala is activated, it shuts down the connection to your clever brain (Neocortex), the part of your brain that reasons and helps you think outside the box and brings new perspectives. That is too demanding to use in a crisis—no matter how much you wish to contact this part of the brain, it's impossible when the Amygdala is in control. That leaves you with three survival strategies: fight, flight, or freeze.

The amygdala controls fear of heights, fear of spiders, fear of water, fear of flying, fear of darkness, and all other phobias.

As we grow up, the Amygdala will record more and more situations that it will help you avoid, and should you be unfortunate enough to end up in a similar situation, it will hijack your brain to help you survive. If we have a very active Amygdala, it is called anciency. When we develop an anciency, the Amygdala grows bigger, and since it needs space, it takes it from the center next to it, the hippocampus—our center for short and long-term memory. The main issue is that we need our memory to help us remember the times when we survived similar situations or the resources we have. And when the hippocampus shrinks, it gets harder to make the Amygdala loosen its grip on our emotions.

Amygdala triggers can be developed all through life. When I told a corporate team about Amygdala, a man had a big "Aha moment." He told me that some time ago, he was traveling on the German motor-way. His wife was driving the car, and suddenly, the icon for low fuel started to flash. She totally panicked. He tried to calm her down by saying there were at least two gallons left in the tank, and he was sure a fuel station would be within a short distance. Nothing worked. She was breathing fast; her face had gone red, and her hands were sweaty. They talked about it afterward, and she just didn't know why she reacted so strongly. With her common sense, she agreed that it was a bit silly. But now I know, he said. My wife told me many years ago that when she was a child in the seventies, she went for a drive with her parents. She was sitting in the back seat. Back then, there were no seatbelts in the back. She was sitting in the middle seat, looking through the two front seats, when she saw the low fuel icon flashing. At the exact same moment, a car crashed into them from behind. The Amygdala now connected the low fuel icon with something dangerous. Fifty years later, while driving on the highway, she didn't think about the incident, but Amygdala did and made sure she would stay alert.

A senior manager shared with me that there had been a break-in at his apartment. He loved his place, but he couldn't sleep after the break-in. He lay awake the whole night, and his nerves were frayed. If there was a sound from the stairway, wind on the window, or a sound he didn't know, he was alert. If it didn't change, he would have to sell his apartment, even though he didn't want to. I told him that he needed to find something that would make him feel safe so that he could tell himself the "safe thing" when he woke up at night. He had to be prepared. He said, "I can say that I have installed the best alarm system, that they already took everything of value, and that I have a baseball bat under my bed." I told him to try it out, and if some of it didn't make him feel safe, he should come up with something else. He did this for two weeks, and then we met again. He looked much more relaxed, and the deep black circles under his eyes were nearly gone. He had done as I told him, and he managed to sleep through the night twice in the two weeks. This was great, and it gave him trust that he could work through the fear and get Amygdala to let go.

Twice a year, I run a nine-day course for business coordinators that is spread over four months. On top of learning a lot of professional skills, there is also a lot of personal growth. One woman told me she lived on a horse farm but was afraid of the dark. She had to walk from the main house to the stalls every morning, and she hated it. She had put up lots of lights, but it didn't help much; darkness was still behind the light. I felt that just giving her a plan wouldn't be enough. Knowing that the brain has a hard time telling the difference between what you visualize and what is real, I gave her a different task. You can use visualization to make your Amygdala lose its grip on situations that are inappropriate. I asked her to sit in her best chair, where she feels safe every day. First, she should just close her eyes and take a few deep breaths. Think of her horses and how much she loves riding. The next day, I asked her to visualize that she was getting up in the morning. It was dark, and she should walk toward the door in her mind. She was only to go as far as she still felt good, then stop and breathe. I asked her to continue day by day and slowly walk toward the door (mentally), but always stop if she felt scared or uncomfortable. Her husband thought it was hilarious that she was sitting in her chair trying to get rid of her fear of darkness. But she continued. On the last day of the course, everybody shared their takeaway. She told us how she had done as I instructed and slowly got closer and closer to the door. Then she opened the door, and a few days later, she visualized that she took a step outside. Gradually, day by day, she came closer to the stall. We all held our breath. She smiled. "I'm not looking forward to going to the stalls, but I'm not scared anymore. I can do it, and I don't mind. And my husband is not teasing me anymore." That was such a gripping moment. She had shown her Amygdala that she could manage and that it didn't need to hijack her brain every single morning. She was relieved and got back her freedom.

You can do the same with any fear you have. You can also use visualization if you are scared of a situation you know you will encounter. Let's say you are going to do a presentation to your CEO. You are afraid. Then, visualize the whole meeting beforehand; in that way, your brain thinks that you have already been to the meeting, and it went well, and it won't tackle you at the actual meeting. Soccer players do this all the time, too. Before going to big games, they visualize themselves kicking a penalty. They do it over and over again. And when it happens, the brain thinks they have done it before, and they don't become scared. If they do get hijacked by Amygdala, that's when they miss big time.

Exercise:

Do you have any Amygdala triggers? (We all do, so be curious.)

- How do you react when the Amygdala takes control?
- Can you tell what triggers your Amygdala?
- If you were to make a plan for the given situation, what can you tell yourself that will make you feel safe?

Remember to make a plan for every amygdala trigger. Create your plans when you are calm and have mental bandwidth, so you can use them when your brain is under pressure.

Things that can also help you when the Amygdala hijacks your brain:

1. Deep breats
2. Meditation and relaxation exercises.

3. Focus on your successes—something that has given you a good feeling.
4. Look for what you know to be true.
5. Do something physical, go for a run, dance, or whatever helps you.
6. Pay attention to what is important to you.

PART III

Your Identity and Core Values
The inner compass

7

WHAT CREATES YOUR IDENTITY?

In my country, most people link their identity to their job, but depending on the culture, people can identify as volunteers, looking after the home and kids, or something else valuable to us. Our identity is deeply rooted in what we find valuable and how we present ourselves.

My youngest son and his best friend since kindergarten started school in the same class. On the first day, I talked to the dad as I have done so many times before. Suddenly, it hit me: I had known him for three years, and we had never discussed where he works. I didn't have any idea of it, and I only knew that he was an accountant. I asked him. He laughed and said that he never told anybody unless they asked. "I'm not proud of where I work," he said. I began to get really curious. "I work in the government tax department." I got it. In recent years, there have been several cases in the news where there have been issues with the government tax department, putting them under a cloud. He just didn't want to be identified as working there. A year later, he approached me and told me he had a new job at a big law firm, and he beamed proudly. The way he walked changed, his car changed, and now he loved talking about his job. A part of his identity changed, and it changed his confidence and how he was in the world, too.

In our personal lives, we have many different "titles," such as mother or father, soccer coach, volunteer, cheerleader, wife, husband, or partner. We can identify ourselves as being rich or poor. Black or white. Gay or straight. Or we can identify with our religion. You could also identify with something that is "special" about you: being artistic, sporty, academic, or focused on how you look. In society, there is a lot of focus on our work, and as soon as anyone tells you what they do, you link it to being valuable or not. If you are unconscious of this, you hold it up against your identity to see who is more worthy. That is why some people play the title card when they need to complain about something and call customer service. "This is Doctor Janson" or "This is lawyer Peter Barrett." But their title has nothing to do with the TV they bought or the complaint they are making; they are using their work identity to state their value. If you are unemployed, it will also have an impact on your identity. Today, many people say they are between jobs instead of unemployed. I have also heard of people who lost their jobs and became consultants without consulting anyone. It all comes back to feeling worthy.

If we solely identify ourselves with our job title, we'll also suffer a greater loss if we're fired or lose our title in some other way.

When we identify with something, we believe it to be the truth. And depending on what we identify with, it can hold more or less value in our society. Lawyers, doctors, and CEOs often have a high status and value in their identity. Whereas politicians, car salespeople, and parking attendants don't. It's often our ego that is highly concerned about the title we hold. For the ego, a prestigious title has a lot of status, and we can feel more worthy. Simultaneously, our titles send signals to the outside world. Since our society is highly oriented toward them, it can provide "free" respect, recognition, social benefits, or hotel and flight upgrades due to having a CEO title.

Titles and work contribute to shaping our identity and, for many, serve as the cornerstone of our identity throughout life. If changes are made to our title or if job functions are rearranged, it always impacts our sense of identity. This is one of the reasons we often take changes personally and might find them difficult. It changes the image we have of ourselves that we present to others. Naturally, it's more difficult for us to lose a title we are happy with than to be promoted. You can also be identified as the best on your team to solve problems or be known as the "go-to" person in the department. You can be a super user of a program, and if that program is dropped, what are you then?

"Our identity gives us a sense of security about who we are. It helps form an impression of our status and what position we hold in society."

-SC

When we build an identity based on our title, abilities, and position in the workplace, we will experience that the foundation is shaking beneath us when changes occur that we don't have control over. It places us in a vulnerable and insecure position and can cause us to feel inadequate or incompetent. The same goes at home. If your identity is linked to your wealth or being married to someone, you will also be vulnerable if those change.

One of my former students told me that her father was the CEO of a big international company, and every day, he went to work as he had done for over 34 years. One day, her mother discovered that he was not actually going to work; he left as if he were. He dressed, grabbed his lunch, took off every morning, and returned at the usual time. But for six months, he had not been working. He had been fired, but he was so embarrassed that he didn't tell anybody and pretended to go to work so nobody would find out. The day her mother confronted him, he hanged himself. It is a tragedy and reveals how deeply rooted we can be in our identity. Never underestimate the meaning of your or other people's identity when you deal with changes. It's an important place to look if there is a lot of resistance to a change, and many people miss the profound impact a change can have on our identity.

A CEO told me he used to work at a worldwide-known brewery, and now he changed jobs to a big parcel company. His friends were surprised. They thought that the brewery was more respected, but he didn't care. At the parcel company, he had more responsibility, and the tasks were more interesting. Another employee from the parcel company told me that she works in customer service, and when she tells people, they are always a bit condescending. Most people think the company is just moving parcels from A to B, but this company does so much for the employees' well-being and growth. She said deep down she didn't care much about titles, but she was still a bit irritated by others reactions. I told her that the next time anyone asked her about her job, she should simply state: I work in the best customer service in the country.

An identity based on our job, social status, or finances can provide security, higher self-worth, and status. But remember, the title itself is essentially "hollow." It's what you attribute to it that matters most.

Use Your Identity to Create a Change.

If you want to make a change in your life, you can use the way you identify yourself as a strong support. Let's say you want to stop smoking. What do you tell others? "I'm trying to quit." Or do you say, "I don't smoke." Even if you haven't completely managed to quit, you're manifesting a new identity that will help you get there. The same goes for any other change. Are you thinking about writing a book, or are you writing a book? It doesn't matter how many pages you have written. Begin to change your identity to what you want to be. I'm not saying that because of that, you will stop smoking and you will write a book, but it can support you on your way to how you see yourself. It affects your self-worth, how you present yourself in the world, and how valuable you feel.

If you are fired or otherwise experience a blow to your identity, it's important that you focus on your skills and strengths, not on your title. It's you as a person who fills the title and gives it value.

When I work with a company going through a merger, there is always an identity fight. If it's not addressed, it can go on for years. "They are from the old Fleet Boston Bank. I'm from Bank of America." I have seen how these labels stick for years if a new identity is not presented in an attractive way. And it can create a division between people that is totally unnecessary.

Our identity at home changes throughout our entire life. We go from being children to teens, young adults, and grown-ups, and some become parents and grandparents. We can also create an identity around illness; when we meet others, that is how we present ourselves. It will influence our lives, but we can change it and let something else be present. Our identity impacts how we feel inside and the way we think about ourselves, so it's important to become aware of all the elements that define our identity.

Write down everything you like about yourself, personally and professionally, what you're good at, what you find enjoyable, and what energizes you. Identify situations where you handled a task well and recognize which of your qualities you used. This will help you build your "true" identity, not one dependent on a workplace and title.

I call it a show-off list. Everybody should have one. Because if you don't know what you're great at and what your strengths are, how can anybody else know?

Exercise:

Make a list of all the things that define your identity:

For example, for me, it would be:

- I'm an author.
- Lecturer
- Speaker
- Mother
- PhD student
- Psychotherapist
- ...

And pay attention to how my list mainly consists of my work identity. It is so powerful in my culture. What about you?

My identity:

Now, make your show-off list.

1.

2.

3.

4.

5.

6.

7.

8.

9.

10.

What would you like to change in your identity?

Next time you present yourself, you will say:

8

THE FOUNDATION OF YOUR IDENTITY

Imagine a house that represents you. The house's foundation says something about how well you are rooted in life and how grounded you are. Your values lie in your foundation. These are what you should build your life upon and uphold throughout life.

Your house is what you present outwardly. You can have a beautiful home with pillars out front and paned windows, a magnificent house that always appears perfect. And so do you. But you might be working overtime because, inside the house, there is chaos, and you don't want others to notice—that's why you work hard to maintain that beautiful façade.

If you've built a house on a foundation made of sand or gravel, your foundation will shift when you face "headwinds," get challenged, or perhaps experience stress. It could mean losing your foothold and having difficulty standing by yourself.

Some people forget to install a front door in their house. It symbolizes that others can overstep their boundaries whenever it suits them. That can be very uncomfortable, and if that's the case, it's important to become aware of it and install a "front door"—with a lock—so you can start setting healthy boundaries.

Some people are also busy fixing others' houses rather than looking at their own. They can be incredibly good at helping others but often use it as an excuse to avoid taking responsibility for their own challenges. It's easier to point out others' faults and shortcomings than to take responsibility for one's own.

A woman attended my personal growth program, and her appearance blew me away. She looked astonishing even though it was early morning, and she was a participant and not the one at the center all day. I later found out that she always looked like that, even if she was going to the bakery at six in the morning. I have never been that fussy about my appearance when I'm not working. Honestly, I don't care how I look when shopping in the morning. I was puzzled and curious about what lay beneath the urge to constantly look perfect. Later, I found out that she had a difficult childhood. She was left at a home for orphans when she was four months old. And she had stayed in several foster homes that didn't work out. She had a strong will to survive and discovered that if she presented herself well, she would be more respected and feel worthy. But inside, she was still the little girl longing for love and care and who just wanted to be seen. She had been fighting for her position in life and now worked as a manager in a bank. She had hidden all the pain in a deep well of darkness inside. Her house was built on a shaky foundation, and every single day, she worked hard to maintain her position.

When you become aware of how much of your identity you invest in your job title and position, you can compare it to your house and what you present to others. Consider whether you are working overtime to hide your weaknesses or lack of skills from others—and, therefore, have built an impressive house that will dazzle most people. In that case, you will always work overtime to maintain your outward façade.

If your foundation isn't solid, your title and place in the world will become hollow, and you'll have to work hard to convince others of your worth.

How to Build a Strong Foundation for Your House

The most important ingredient in our foundation is our core values. Core values are the three things you won't compromise on in your life. Unfortunately, many people are unaware of their core values and do not know what to stand up for. When we don't know our core values, we often follow others and are unsure about what is truly important to us. A core value can vary depending on what is valuable to you. There are hundreds of different values, most of them qualities we contain or see in others and would like to own. The most common values are love, respect, trust, freedom, creativity, and health. On sagarconstantin.com/byor, you can sign up for free and get access to a list of values. Knowing your core values makes it much easier to follow your heart, set healthy boundaries, and stand up for yourself. You can become more true to yourself and what matters to you instead of trying to please others or battle low self-esteem. If you are tired of fighting for your place in the world and want to be respected, you must become aware of your core values. Then you will know the most important thing to you, and don't compromise.

One of my core values is love. Knowing that, I can now define what this value means to me. The definition can differ from person to person even though the value is the same. A definition helps the values come to life and become valuable. If you know your value is love and nothing more, it won't do you any good. It will just be an empty word. You might have a husband and children, but you work late hours every single day, and when you come home, you also work at night. And if you are with your family, you are not present; your thoughts are somewhere else. You don't prioritize time with your family, so your value is worthless, and it doesn't fill you up and bring meaningfulness to your life. My definition of love as my value is: *Spending time with my family and friends where we are present and doing things we all enjoy.* Now, my value has direction and behavior attached to it. I know how to honor my value and make it come alive. I wouldn't know that if it was just *love*. My value is valuable and brings energy and a deep sense of meaning to my life.

Fall and winter are always my busy seasons, and I am on the road a lot to give speeches and lectures. When my core value is *love*, I know my priority is to get home, if possible, or not to have too many plans other than being with my family on weekends. Let's say a friend calls me and asks if I want to take a first-class trip to New York. I wouldn't think twice if I weren't aware of my values. I would say yes right away. I love New York, and I love traveling first class. On the plane, while sipping champagne, I would suddenly hear myself complaining about the quality of the champagne or that the seats weren't as comfortable as I expected. When walking the streets of New York, I would point out how annoying it is to have so many people in one place. I would project my frustration of not being true to myself onto the external circumstances or someone else. It could also lead to starting a fight with my friend about something that didn't matter, like which route to take or when to visit certain shops. We all do that unconsciously. Knowing my core values and having defined them, I know my priority is my family. So, the answer wouldn't be hard: "Thank you for asking. I would love to know if we can move the trip to January?" If that weren't possible, the choice would still be easy. I would say no thank you and wouldn't regret my decision at all; I had been faithful to my values and myself.

"Values are like an inner compass that guides us through life according to our soul's purpose."
-SC

When you live according to your values, you will always be on the right path and save yourself from detours that cause you to lose yourself and your direction in life. You will be more authentic, and your life will be based on the things that make it meaningful.

A German psychologist, Victor Frankl, was sent to Auschwitz during World War II and survived the horror. After the war, he began to study why some people survived while others didn't. He discovered that the people who could find meaning in life, like finding their loved ones after the war or helping others, carried themselves differently and were more determined to survive.

A meaningful life begins with knowing what is valuable to you. Knowing your core values will help you make choices that will make you happy and satisfied not just now but for the rest of your life.

Meaning is what gets us out of bed in the morning, and knowing your core values will support you in being truer to yourself every day for the rest of your life.

Once you have discovered your core values, they don't change. It doesn't matter if you find them when you are twenty or sixty, they will be the same. Our values are rooted deep in our souls, and finding your values is a shortcut to getting closer to your soul's purpose. When you begin to look for your core values, it's like peeling an onion. First, you find some values, and then you see there are some deeper layers. One of my values has been personal growth for many years. Lately, I have discovered that there is a deeper layer to it. Awareness. Everything I do is about creating awareness—my teaching, my books, and my way of life. When you find your core value, it is like striking a pure, clear tone that resonates. Let's say you find your core values when you're young, and one of them is freedom. When you are young, your definition of your value might be: I want the freedom to live and work where it feels good. So, you are on a contract and have a lease. Then you meet someone, and you have children and buy a house. Now, your definition needs to change to match your life and new priorities. You look at your value and redefine your definition. Now, it's not possible to do whatever you want when you want. You have different responsibilities. Now, freedom can be defined as having time by yourself every single day, and maybe it's just thirty minutes, but you need your thirty minutes to feel good. If you don't have the time by yourself where you can do what you feel like, you will begin to work late, walk the dog, or come up with excuses to stay out late. I have a friend who started to hide in the petrol station just to get time by himself. When the kids grow up, you might regain more freedom, and eventually, you'll have days where you can do whatever you feel like. If you are not aware of your values and honor them, you will go into survival mode and do what is needed to get a bit of your value fulfilled. When you know your core values, you can talk to your family and let them know so you can support each other. When you tell your partner that you need freedom, and that means time by yourself, she will understand that you are not rejecting her; it is a deep need you have in order to be true to yourself.

When you are aware of your values and stand firm on your solid foundation, it is much easier to deal with any change or challenge in your life.

Finding Your Core Values:

1. To begin exploring what your core values are, you can start by making a list of everything important to you. Just brainstorm and write it all down.
2. After you do that, look for values in what you have written down. You can use the list of values to help you. If you have written: Going for a walk in the forest. The value can be nature or exercise. Make sure to have single words that are your value, not sentences.
3. If you have some values that are the same, you can group them. It can be family, friends, children, and love. It is all the same value. Be careful not to group values that are not the same, like respect and trust.
4. Now look at everything you wrote down and find the values you would be willing to fight for and put them aside —these are the ones that are most valuable to you. Next, you can begin to remove those that are nice to have but not

something you will fight for. See if you can narrow your list down to three to five values.

Here is an example.

Answering the question: What is important to you? Here is what I would say:

Freedom, trust, eating healthy, exercise, my family and friends, love, teaching, writing books, spending time with my boys, traveling, adventure, awareness, spirituality, reading, being curious... and I could go on and on.

First, some of them are the same value. Family, friends, kids, and love are the same value. So, I decided which word to use to cover them all. My word is LOVE. Awareness and spirituality are also the same values. Here, I chose Awareness.

Then my list would look like this:

Freedom, trust, eating healthy, exercise, love, teaching, writing books, traveling, adventure, awareness, reading, curiosity.

You will most likely have many more words; this is just an example. From this list, I now need to ask myself, which are the most important ones I wouldn't do without? And which ones are nice to have but not worth fighting for?

Now, my list will get smaller. These are the most important ones to me:

Freedom, trust, love, teaching, writing books, awareness.

I have narrowed it down to six. If I look at teaching and ask myself if it is any kind of teaching, the answer is no. When I look deeper, awareness is the key to my teaching. So, in order to enjoy teaching, I need to teach some kind of awareness.

Awareness is the pivot of everything I do. That also means that awareness is my core value and is included in all my lectures, books, and spirituality.

That leaves me with four core values: *Love, trust, freedom, and awareness.*

The next step is to define each one so you know exactly how to honor them and bring them to life.

If you want to begin searching for your values, set an alarm for ten minutes and then ask yourself: What is important to you? Begin writing it down. Try to stick to words, not long sentences. When the ten minutes are up, continue as I described above until you have three core values, and then define them.

When you have found your core values, remember to make decisions that are true to them and observe if it makes you happy to do so. If it doesn't, it is because you haven't found the right values yet. It can take time.

If you want to know your core values, I have made an online course you can access for free. Just head to sagarconstantin.com/byor and sign up.

PART IV

The Human Control Center
Understanding yourself and others

9

CREATING A BUFFER ZONE

Whenever there is an action, there is also a reaction. Usually, we react right away and do as we always do. It might not be the best reaction or thing to do, but we respond instantly, giving ourselves no time to think or reflect. Many people wish they were able to stop and think before they react but find it hard to do so. We often aren't free to do what is more appropriate in the situation, so we react on instinct.

Creating what I call a buffer zone can be very helpful. It will help you reflect before you react and give you the freedom to do what is best in the situation. The buffer zone is a short break that allows you to see what you usually do and what you can do instead. To build your own inner buffer zone, the first step is to take a breath before saying anything or reacting. This is not easy, and you need to be aware of it first and then practice.

As you breathe in, you shift your attention to how you feel. Are you tired, upset, or under pressure? What is your inner state? Just notice.

Then, zoom out and look at the other person. What is their situation? Are they under pressure? What do they need? Imagine you are on an island, and they are on a different island. You look at your island first, then jump over to the other island and look around. Now, you understand your situation and their situation. When I told a friend about the buffer zone, she said that at her workplace, they use:

Pause ▶ Reflect ▶ Zoom out

Pause to take a breath. Reflect on your emotions and situation. Zoom out and see the greater perspective. This will strengthen your buffer zone and give you the freedom to make the best and most conscious choice in any situation. And it doesn't take long when you make it a habit to say Pause—Reflect—Zoom out.

10

UNDERSTAND YOUR BRAIN, UNDERSTAND YOURSELF

Our brain has been developed over millions of years. The first part of the brain that was created is the reptile brain. This is the most primitive part of our brain, and we share this part of the brain with animals like sharks, lizards, and rays. For most people, the reptile brain kicks in when we are challenged, experience a change, or are under pressure. The challenge is the way we handle situations with this part of the brain. We aim to survive and don't have the ability to use our common sense or have a constructive conversation. We rely solely on our instincts. The reptile brain controls fight, flight, freeze, sex, hunger, and sleep (drives and instincts). This means that if we perceive a change as threatening, it's this part of the brain we are likely to use to deal with the situation. We are not always aware of our inner state and can be unaware that this part of the brain takes control. In this part of the brain, there is no reasoning or common sense, only fight, flight, or freeze. We are more likely to use this part of the brain when we are tired or stressed out because it's easy and nearly free of charge to use.

One hundred thousand years ago, humans used the reptilian brain to survive on the savannah when facing life-threatening situations. The brain is wired to help us survive and will constantly be on guard against danger. That's also why many instinctively look for the negative aspects of a change to assess if it might be "dangerous." At home, small things can instantly grow big and seem overwhelming because you are tired and out of energy. It could be your partner inviting guests over without you knowing, and you are not in the mood for it and would rather lie on the couch. It can be that you are out of milk or simply feeling rejected. At work, a change of tasks, a new manager, or being late to a meeting because of a traffic block can make us use the reptile brain rather than a more sensible part of the brain.

The fight response is directed chiefly outward. You are in the kitchen making dinner, and something smells burnt; at the same time, your partner approaches you and asks a question, and you answer instantly and harshly. You push him away to survive and save the food. You are under pressure and don't have the surplus to connect with reasoning and tell him nicely to wait. If he is unaware of why you react as you do, he will jump right into his reptile brain, too, and reply with a fight, flight or freeze response. An answer could be, "Relax, what is the matter with you!" That is the typical beginning of a conflict. If he recognized that you were under pressure, he could stay calm and ask if you were all right or needed help instead of pushing you further over the edge. When I ask my students which one of them is their favorite to use, most people reply fight. The fight response is the most outgoing survival mechanism, and when using it, the brain believes that it's better to hit before getting hurt in order to survive.

Flight mode is the one we often use to avoid a conflict or where we hope things will pass so we don't have to deal with them. We don't engage, and we don't make decisions. We avoid other people and pretend that we are not there. Let's say a friend asks if you want to go to the movies. You are tired and not up for it. Instead of answering, you pretend that you haven't seen the message. Flight mode. If they call you and ask you on the phone, you might try to change the subject and, in that way, avoid the question and hang up. We use the reptile brain so much more than we are aware of, and we do it to avoid confrontation. Many people don't want to take responsibility, so it's easier to walk away from the matter or pretend they haven't heard. With a higher information load and access to news and social media, many people will use their reptile brain a lot more since they are tired, and it's easier to use the flight response than to get involved. Another way to use flight mode is if you want to avoid something at home and swiftly go out for a walk with the dog... again. My twelve-year-old son always uses flight mode after dinner when we need to clear the table. People can also disappear into watching a series or sport on TV to avoid pain inside or something happening in their life —anything that can help shift the attention away from whatever is confronting them.

I know that my favorite way to react under pressure is to use the fight response. But some time ago, I was invited to a 50th birthday party held by three people, and I knew two of them. I hadn't seen them for many years and was looking forward to seeing them again. It was at the end of summer, and the evenings had begun to be a bit chilly. I knew the party would be outdoors, and I made sure to bring a jumper. Leading up to the day, I had a lot of lectures, and on the day of the party, I held a webinar for two hours with 150 leaders attending from all over the world, and it was also translated into Spanish and Portuguese. My social energy was gone; honestly, I just wanted to spend the evening on my couch. But I went. When I got there, I spoke to the two people I knew and realized I didn't know anyone else. At dinner, I talked to a nice stranger, and after dinner, another one. It was only eight o'clock, and I was both tired and without any interest in talking to more people I didn't know. A woman came up to me; she was really nice, and it turned out we had a lot in common. We spoke for half an hour, and I was getting so cold. So, I said, "I'm just going to go and grab a jumper from the car," and left. The next thing I realized was that I was driving away from the party. I stopped in the middle of the road and began to laugh. I realized that I was fleeing. My instincts were driving the car. I heard myself saying: "You can turn around and go back. It is not very grown-up to leave a party without saying goodbye." While arguing with myself, my survival instinct had ordered my foot to hit the pedal and begin to drive, and before I knew it, I was on my couch watching TV. I couldn't help laughing at myself. Even though I talk about these mechanisms every single day, they can also take control of me. The next day, I wrote my friends a note explaining why I left and said I hoped they would invite me again when they turned 60.

I'm so amazed to see how our brains work in so many ways and determine how we react and make choices. The important thing is that we become aware of it and then can make a choice from a better place. In my case, there were also emotions at stake. I hate being the center of attention when I'm tired, and if I were to say goodbye, I knew people would say, why are you leaving already? Stay a bit longer —and I would attract too much attention. My survival instinct made me flee, and my emotions supported it. Common sense would definitely have said something different. When we are tired and under pressure, it is so important that we pay attention to these mechanisms so we don't end up in situations where we or other people get hurt.

In the news, you sometimes hear about a hit-and-run car accident in which people leave the crime scene even though the other person needs help. This is not because they reflect and decide it is the best thing to do. It's their instinct based on history and fear.

Freeze can also be hard to deal with. When people freeze, their brain shuts down. The connection to the center for reason cuts off. You cannot contact that part of the brain when you freeze. That is also why people struggle in exams and forget everything they learned. They can't connect to the clever part of the brain when it shuts down. When you freeze, it is like you are an empty shell with no thoughts or ability to move.

Imagine you are on the African savannah, and a big saber-toothed tiger appears. You freeze and hope it walks right past you. We do the same in meetings when asked a question we are not sure of or if something unexpected happens. It is hard to have a conversation with a person who has frozen, and it is easy to become upset. They are not answering. And you get even more irritated. I call the freeze state playing dead. Imagine you are in a meeting, and your manager asks if anyone would be responsible for the team-building event. Everybody sits completely still with fixed gazes. One looks down, another looks out the window, and a third avoids eye contact. They are playing dead, hoping not to be seen. It's so funny when you begin to realize when other people (and yourself, too) are playing dead. It's just a simple survival mechanism to avoid more work or having to provide an answer to something you are not sure about. We can also play dead at home; when you ask your kids to set the table, they don't answer. They hope it will go away if they pretend they are dead. If you ask if they want an ice cream, they are suddenly brought back to life. The best way to deal with people playing dead is to address it. It is hard to get away with playing dead if someone sees what you are doing. This goes for any inappropriate behavior; when you call it out, you can talk about it, and it is hard to continue doing it. I sometimes

SAGAR CONSTANTIN

experience whole teams playing dead or participants at a lecture when they become tired. If I ask them a question there is no reaction at all. Then, I know it's time for a break or exercise.

Freeze can happen at any time or place, often when you least expect it. In accidents, you hear about people who didn't help a victim; they just stood there and did nothing. Their brain is shut down. Afterward, they can't believe they didn't do anything, but their whole body froze at that moment.

No matter which of the three survival mechanisms you use, there is one thing that can support you or a person who feels under attack. Try to create some sense of safety. Don't push the person or demand an answer. Give them support and, for example, ask them something that is not dangerous that can shift their focus. In an exam situation, you can help by asking the student about something where they feel comfortable or just for a second talk about something completely different, like their dog or how they got to the university. At work, you can ask your colleague if you should get a cup of coffee or take a break outside. If they freeze in a presentation or the PowerPoint doesn't work, support them by removing the attention from them by taking the lead on a question or suggestion. When you realize another person is using fight, flight, or freeze, you know they will never have a constructive conversation or resolve an issue until they get out of it. Stop and help them back to a safe place. If that doesn't work, take a break and walk away. Never just walk away without saying why you are walking away. Always say you need a break; don't put it on them, as it will just worsen the situation.

The three last instincts, sex, hunger, and sleep, are also familiar to most people—makeup sex after an argument, eating when feeling challenged, and feeling tired when facing difficulty in your life. I remember when I did my psychotherapist training, the therapist told us that no matter how exhausted we felt, we weren't allowed to sleep during the day. I thought it was a bit strange at the time, and some people didn't listen. They had such an urge to sleep. Now, I know it was a way to escape whatever they were facing inside.

We all have all six instincts, but most have a favorite—one we tend to aim for first, and if it doesn't work, we use one of the others. It can depend on the person or situation. If the person in front of us has a higher status, our leader, a CEO, or an authority, we are more likely to use flight or freeze. In order to use the fight response toward a person with a higher status than we have, we need a high amount of psychological safety. That is why children dare to shout at their parents; they feel safe. We are more likely to use the fight response if we feel equal or have a higher status than another person. But some people never fight no matter who they are facing. Our reaction can also depend on the situation. Is it life-threatening? Did you make a mistake? Are you under pressure, or is there something you fear?

When we become aware of which survival mechanisms we use the most, we can begin to practice taking a breath before reacting and, in that way, gain freedom of choice. Will I continue or will I do something different and more appropriate? Pause—Reflect—Zoom out. When you are presented with a difficult situation, remember to observe if you are challenged before judging or reacting. That way, it will be easier to hear what is said and ask the most suitable questions.

Some people use all the survival mechanisms frequently, and some stick to one or two. And, like me, you can have a favorite and be surprised by your reaction.

Exercise:

Which survival mechanism is your favorite?

What do you do when you are under pressure and someone challenges you?

- Can you identify situations where you have been fighting?
- Can you identify situations where you have been fleeing?
- Can you identify situations where you have been freezing?
- Can you identify situations where you have used sex as a survival mechanism?
- Can you identify situations where you have used sleep as a survival mechanism?
- Can you identify situations where you have used hunger as a survival mechanism?

The more curious you are, the easier it will be to start recognizing your own strategies and change them for the better.

11

THE LIMBIC SYSTEM

The next part of the brain developed is the Limbic system. The limbic system controls our emotions. It is also where we get a sense of reality and consciousness. The limbic system is fast and cheap to use. The brain uses glucose to function; like the reptile brain, this system doesn't need much to run. There are many different opinions on whether thoughts are faster than emotions or vice versa. In my research and working with people for over twenty-five years, I have found that it is not a simple question to answer since many things play a role. However, as a guideline, I will always say emotions come first, then thoughts, and and following that, behavior. You can think of something and recall an emotion, but the emotion has already been linked to that thought earlier. Emotions are fast, and as you will see later in the book, it also depends on the thought. Is it a thought, or is it common sense? There is a difference: reasoning is connected to another part of the brain, and the distance to reasoning is longer than the distance to thoughts you are familiar with. When dealing with challenges, it's good to be aware of the triggered emotions and see what thoughts you put on top of them to justify your behavior. When dealing with a challenge, many people only care about the thoughts and don't realize that the emotion will keep pushing you back when you try to move forward or keep you in a place—good or bad, so you don't make real progress.

We share the limbic system with animals like cats, horses, and dogs. Dogs have the most developed limbic system after humans. Many dogs are highly emotionally intelligent. If you have a dog, you have most likely experienced that your dog has reacted if you have been upset, stressed, or sad. They feel it immediately and will try to help you balance your limbic system. Cats are also emotionally intelligent, and they, too, sense how their human is feeling and often react to it. You might have heard the term being a horse-whisperer. Some people say it's bogus, but it's not. They use emotions to communicate and balance emotions. If you are upset and you get on a horse, the horse will feel it immediately and react to it. In Denmark, dogs are used in retirement homes to support the elderly. When a dog lies close to you, it can help regulate your nervous system. Our nervous system is developed from birth, but not until the age of six to seven months are we capable of regulating our nervous system. We depend on another person or being to help us. We learn to regulate the nervous system by being close to others—skin-to-skin. Therefore, it is crucial for a small child's development to have a lot of skin contact with a person who is in balance so they can learn to regulate their nervous system. When we grow older and are challenged, our nervous system will be under pressure, and the better we are at regulating it, the easier it will be for us to cope with stress and prevent being stressed. This is called resilience. Resilience means the ability to balance your nervous system. This also means that the foundation for being good at dealing with challenges when you are an adult is laid when you are an infant. When the child grows up, it still needs support in regulating the nervous system. I have met several parents who have told me that their child has ADHD. They have a dog, and when the dog senses that the child is challenged, it lies next to the child and helps regulate the child's nervous system. And it works.

Not many people are aware of how crucial feeling safe is for infants' development and how much it influences our capacity to deal with emotions and change as adults.

Emotions

Humans have seven basic emotions: Anger, Fear, Sadness, Surprise, Happiness, Disgust, and Shame. All the emotions have underlying emotions that can also be activated. As you can see, most of the emotions are "negative." It is important to say that I believe that all emotions are equally important to us, and an emotion is neither good or bad. When working with emotions, it's all about becoming friends with the emotion and, in that way, being able to contain it instead of shutting it down, throwing it at someone else, or hoping it will go away. When I say negative, it's because Anger, Fear, Sadness, Disgust, and Shame don't bring joy to many people. They challenge us and can be hard to deal with. Surprise can be positive or negative, depending on the situation. When you open your Christmas presents, you don't know if they will be good or bad... And happiness is the only purely positive emotion we have. One can wonder why that is, and the answer is simple. Our brains are developed to survive, and if we had an excess of positive emotions, we wouldn't evolve as humans and wouldn't survive. Negative emotions help us stay alert to dangerous situations and deal with them. However, research in positive psychology has also shown us that today, we can benefit greatly from positive emotions and focusing on our strengths to deal with difficult situations. We can train our brain to act more positively and, in that way, use our positive emotions and make the negative ones less active.

Train Your Brain To Be More Positive

If you moan a lot and often look for the things you don't like or are unhappy about, it can be beneficial to begin to reshape your brain. The brain is plastic and can be shaped throughout life. Children's brains are more plastic than adults, so they learn faster. Our brain's plasticity depends on how good we are at maintaining plasticity. If we often make changes and challenge ourselves with new tasks and knowledge, our brains will stay fit. If we don't, it will be much harder to make changes and understand others when needed.

The brain is wired by paths of emotions, thoughts, and behavior. There are positive and negative paths that light up on a brain scan in the prefrontal cortex. When we have predominantly negative paths in the brain, we are more likely to look for what we don't like about a situation and feel resistance. If we have more positive paths in the brain, we will look for opportunities and take responsibility in a challenging situation.

You can begin to use a few simple techniques to make your brain more positive. Whenever something challenges you, ask yourself—how can I take responsibility, what are the possibilities, and what can I learn from this? In this way, you activate the positive paths in your brain and maintain them, too. If you want to create more positive paths in the brain, the best way to do so is to be grateful. Gratitude not only supports the existing paths but helps you expand the number of positive paths, and in that way, it will be easier to stay positive and open when you experience a change.

––––––––––

Exercise:

Are you mainly positive or negative?

- How can you shift your focus and look for possibilities instead of limitations?
- Where can you show gratitude and to whom?

12

BECOMING EMOTIONALLY INTELLIGENT

Emotional intelligence is the ability to recognize, manage, and understand both your own emotions and those of others. Emotional intelligence gives us the ability to be empathic, caring, and able to create healthy relationships. It's all about understanding and using your emotions in a healthy way that supports you in having a better relationship with yourself and others.

We all have the same range of emotions, but some people are not familiar with all of them. Many people learn from their childhood to shut down emotions. If you trip and hurt your knee, your dad might have said, there is nothing to cry over; don't be such a wimp. In that instant, you learned that your emotion was wrong and it was better to hide it away. It could also be that you became angry while playing a game, and your mother said, stop it; there is no reason to be angry—it's just a game. But you wanted to win and made a mistake that upset you. To you, that is a good reason to be angry. But you shut it down. The more we close our emotions when we are children, the harder it is to reconnect as adults. Some people are totally disconnected and cannot feel anything. For most people, it is possible to reconnect if given the proper help and support. It takes time, and you must be persistent.

In many cultures, we learn to control our emotions. It has a backside since we are working overtime to keep an eye out for situations that can activate an emotion we don't want. It's like putting an emotion in a beach ball and then trying to hold it underwater so no one sees it. It takes up your energy. Often, you don't just have one beach ball but two or three to look after. And when you go out for drinks, it's much harder to keep the balls underwater, and suddenly, an emotion slips out, and you don't know what to do. You feel insecure and afraid of the other person's reaction. A change can also trigger an emotion and a loss of control, which can be why we fight the change.

Being Identified

Becoming more emotionally intelligent means that you can also shift from being identified with an emotion to being unidentified. When you are identified with an emotion, you believe the emotion is the whole truth. You are one with the emotion, and your entire point of view is colored by the emotion as if a filter was placed in front of your eyes. When you communicate, you talk through the emotion, and your perception of the world is made through the emotion. It's like adding a filter to your photos; the whole picture changes. There is rarely just one emotion in play, so you can add several filters to your point of view without being aware of it. Let's say a removal truck just pulled up outside where you live. If your attention goes to the street and you begin to wonder who is moving in or out, is it your neighbor or the annoying man down the street? Your thoughts are present with the mover and the truck. Your brain is occupied with the event outside. But if you instead observe the mover and stay present with yourself, then you are not identified. The same goes for emotions. If you can observe the emotion and not let it overtake your whole perspective, it's easier to stay present and act from a neutral place inside you. Then, you don't need to throw the emotion on someone else because you have difficulty containing it.

Becoming Friends with Your Emotions

When you work with your emotions, you can become friends with them. Instead of shutting them down, you open up to them. When something is painful or uncomfortable, trying to get rid of it is natural. But if we always shut down our emotions, we don't get to know them, and then we have an enemy inside us. Initially, it can be hard to breathe into your emotions, but imagine if you meet an old friend you haven't seen for years. In the beginning, it might be a bit awkward, but after some time, you are back in a good place together. It's the same with your emotions. They have been with you your whole life; now it's time to get to know them so they don't tackle you or prevent you from living fully.

When we experience difficult times, getting caught up in an emotion is easy. When you get to know your emotions, you don't need to be afraid of how they feel or act out. They are a part of you. When you don't become identified with them, they don't control you anymore.

There is usually more than one emotion active inside you. If you are curious, you will see. We usually only focus on one emotion and think it's the whole truth. Then, we miss the bigger picture. When you identify with an emotion, you tend to hold on to it longer than necessary. Some people can be stuck in an emotion for days, some-times months, and even years. When you are not afraid of your emotions, you can begin to face them and become friends.

When my grandmother passed away, my mother and her sisters got into a fight. There were eight sisters, each with a different take on how the inheritance should be divided between them. My grand-mother had always helped the ones that needed help. She was an amazing woman, full of positive energy and support. The battle had already begun before she died, and my mother had mentioned it to her because she was so frustrated. She and one of her sisters went to see my grandmother every single day. They took her on trips and cooked for her so she didn't have to move into a retirement home, which she didn't want to do. The other sisters only came to see her occasionally, even though one of them lived just around the corner. My mother and one of her sisters have always been poor but never complained. To them, helping out my grandmother gave them so much joy. My grandmother was supporting them with a little bit of money every month. When the other sisters found out, they wanted my grandmother to sign a piece of paper where it said that the money they had received should be deducted from their part of the inheri-tance. My grandmother was furious and decided to disinherit them. My mother talked her out of it. She knew it would make the whole situation worse. When my grandmother passed away, the rest of the sisters got so greedy that it was too much for my mother and her sister. They haven't spoken to them since. Inheritance, especially, can bring out emotions, and when people identify with what they believe to be the truth, it usually ends up in a conflict.

Exercise:

Begin to observe your emotions when a change happens or something triggers you.

Don't judge or shut them down. Try breathing into them and getting to know them. Let your emotions become friends instead of enemies.

This way, you will take the first important steps to becoming more emotionally intelligent.

13

NEOCORTEX

The last part of the brain we have developed is the Neocortex. Neo means new, and Cortex means brain. The Neocortex is a part of the prefrontal cortex located in our forehead. This is the part of the brain that sets us apart from other mammals—the clever brain. This part of the brain involves reasoning, analyzing, and advanced brain processes. We use this part of the brain to think outside of the box. It's expensive to use, and therefore, some people don't use it. Unfortunately, the brain has a saying: Use it or lose it. If you don't use this part of the brain, it will shrink. In the next chapter, we will look at how you can use and maintain it.

Researchers have found that one of the reasons people get dementia is that they stop using this part of the brain.

When we are challenged in life, the physical distance in our brain from emotion to action is shorter than from emotion to the Neocortex. That is also the reason we sometimes act on a feeling instead of taking a moment to think about it.

We use the Neocortex to deal with changes, and if we want a lasting change in our lives, it is crucial that we use the Neocortex to plan and execute it. A lasting change is possible when we are aware of both feelings and the Neocortex.

There are many different opinions about the capacity of the Neocortex; most researchers agree that it is limited due to the demanding effort to use it. If you want more capacity in your Neocortex, the only way researchers have discovered is meditation. When we meditate, we are present, observing our thoughts, emotions, and body. It's that simple. In doing so, we also set the brain free, which can expand the Neocortex's resources. People who have meditated a lot experience greater calmness and find it easier to differentiate between feelings they have and feelings other people have. They also experience more energy and find it easier to navigate challenging situations.

You can begin to meditate at any time. It's not complicated, and you don't need to sit down for an hour and think of nothing. If you live in a place with a staircase, this is a great place to begin practicing. When you go up the stairs, go slow and focus all your attention on your foot on the stairs. Breathe and walk slowly up the stairs as you focus on your feet. If your mind drifts or you get distracted, don't give up. Come back and continue. Do this once a day. Now, you will begin to feel the presence and observe your body, thoughts, and emotions as you walk up the stairs. Try to walk a little faster when you can walk without being distracted. The better you get, the more complicated things you can do without losing your meditative state. If you have a dog, you can also practice while walking your dog. Do the same as before. Pay attention to your feet landing on the ground. Walk slow. Maybe you can do it for two seconds before your mind begins to talk to you. Maybe you can do ten seconds. How long doesn't matter; what matters is that you start.

You can also help your brain stay healthy by taking a break now and again when you are working. Our brains are overloaded with information and work, and if we want a healthy brain, we need to look after it. The best way to keep your brain fit is to learn new things, exercise, get a good night's sleep, eat healthily, get fresh air, and take breaks.

The Brain's Change System

In 2011, Daniel Kahneman wrote a book called *Thinking, Fast and Slow*, in which he introduced the brain's systems 1 and 2. This knowledge is crucial if you want to succeed with changes and challenges in your life, whether big or small, at home or at work.

In our **System 1** is everything you know already: your memory, experiences, habits, routines, and fingertip knowledge. It's fast and cheap to use. Therefore, many people use it most of the time since it's easier to do what you know by heart rather than try something new. System 1 is the lazy system, and when we use this system, we do as we always have done and cut corners. We stick to our opinions no matter if new information comes to light or others try to enlighten us. System 1 is nearly free of charge, and you will never run out of capacity in this system. We are more likely to use this system when we are tired in the afternoon, have too many tasks, or feel stressed. The reptile brain and the limbic system are connected to System 1.

A great friend of mine works in HR at a huge tech company, and she tried to get the employees to attend self-development and meditation courses to help them work smarter and take care of themselves. It was a struggle; they didn't have time because they already worked 70 hours a week. But are those hours efficient? Are they thinking outside the box and making good decisions? My guess would be no. Nobody can work that many hours and do quality work the whole time. When we get tired, we make poor decisions based on what we already know and are not critical of new information. We don't bother reading emails carefully and rely on what we think they say. And if we are in doubt about something and need to check it with a colleague, we don't if it's not easy. A simple obstacle might be that we don't have their number or that they don't answer the first time we reach out. We become lazy in our judgment and rely on feelings and primitive thinking. Working that many hours is not brain-smart, and the efficiency is low. Taking breaks and working fewer hours while your brain is efficient would be way more beneficial.

When a company must hire many new employees, it usually looks at professional and people skills and ensures that they fit the position. But if the people conducting the interviews become tired, they will begin to rely on whether they like a candidate or a gut feeling. Or they might look at their CV and decide they are perfect for the position without considering which personality type they are or if they will fit into the team dynamic. Many of our decisions during the day are made from the lazy System 1; if we are not aware, we will make decisions that don't do us or anyone else any good.

"People are often hired based on their professional skills and fired due to a lack of human skills."

-SC

We all know the basic health advice. Eat healthy, get a good night's sleep, take a break now and again, exercise, and get some fresh air. But what do we do when we are under pressure? We fall back on System 1. We eat fast food, sleep fewer hours, skip breaks (we tell ourselves we don't have time), and we don't have time to exercise. That can wait. Can you see the picture? We do what is easy for the lazy brain.

System 2 holds the ability to think outside the box, learn new things, and use common sense. This is also where you learn new habits and routines, manage changes, learn new skills, and deal with demanding challenges. Whatever you want to change in your life, you need to access System 2 to succeed. If you don't, you will fall back on your lazy System 1 and your old habits. This is where many people fail when they want to make a change; they plan it from System 1, execute it from System 1, and then don't understand why they fail.

The Neocortex is connected to System 2. This system is expensive to use, and it is limited in capacity. I have heard many different takes on how many hours and minutes you can use this system in a day, and I believe there is no correct answers that fits all. But we don't have unlimited access to System 2. Most people can access it between thirty minutes and one hour a day. Mind you, we jump in and out of system 2, so we don't use it all in one go. We can stretch it so it lasts until lunch, and then we get some sugar in our food, have a break, and access it a bit more for an hour or two. Most people don't have any System 2 capacity left after that. Try to observe for yourself: when are you challenging yourself using System 2, and when are you falling back on your routines in System 1? One thing I can say for sure is that we don't have as much capacity in System 2 as we hope or believe we do. If we did, the world would be quite different. We usually jump into System 2 (our clever brain), get an idea or a new take on a matter, and then jump back into System 1 and connect the dots with something we already know. It can be a matter of seconds that we use System 2 and think outside the box. From my experience and observation in my 24 years as a lecturer, I can say that by two p.m., hardly anyone has any capacity left in their System 2. By that time of day, most people rely on what they already know. When it comes to dealing with changes, making important decisions, and learning, it is essential that we can access our System 2; otherwise, we will fall back into old patterns and continue to do as we have always done.

During the Covid lockdown, I did many online courses and didn't have to travel. It gave me time to translate three of my novels from Danish to English (*The Life*, *The Ring*, and *The Hope*). I had to use my System 2 to translate since it takes quite a lot more skills and knowledge to translate a fiction book than to teach subjects I know by heart and knowledge that is stored in my System 1. For two years, I watched how I shifted from one system to another when translating. From around 8 a.m. until 12 p.m., I could translate ten to twelve pages. In the afternoon, I never succeeded in translating more than four to five pages. And it wasn't because I didn't want to; that would have made the whole process faster, but in the afternoon, I couldn't find the words or remember basic things I had worked on in the morning. Once, I even gave one of my main characters a new eye color. I was amazed to see how big a difference there was in my work's quality and efficiency. I sometimes found myself staring at the screen in the afternoon, thinking that if I kept staring, something great would appear. It never did. I discovered it was much better to go for a walk on the beach or ride my bike—then, an idea or a solution to a problem would appear.

I meet people who like to challenge the fact that we can't learn new things all day. What about school kids or young people who go to university? Younger kids have more plasticity in their brains, meaning they learn faster. The older you get, the less plasticity there is in your brain. For young people at university, having lectures at five in the afternoon takes a very inspiring professor to teach them anything. The brain will always grab something new and jump back to System 1 and try to fit it with something you know already, and in that way, we might experience that we learn new things all day, but the truth is that we learn a few new things and connect it with some previous experience. When I ask my students how many hours and minutes they use their System 2 in a whole day, many reply that it is four to six hours, and it feels like that. We are solving issues and developing new systems. We are attending meetings and making decisions. But honestly, are you using System 1 or 2?

To make a change in our lives, we need to activate System 2. In System 2, we practice the change and learn; when we master the change, we move it into System 1. How long we need to practice in System 2 depends on the change and our ability to deal with the change. Some changes are easy to implement, and others can take years. When people fall back into old behavior, it is simply because they haven't stayed long enough in System 2. It is easier and more tempting to fall back into old patterns, especially when you get tired or bored with the change.

I see it so often. People want to lose weight. They find a diet and stick to it for weeks or months. When they either get demotivated, give up, or reach their goal, they fall back into their old eating habits, and before long, all that was lost is now regained and sometimes a bit more. Knowing how the brain works, we can understand why it is so hard to change habits or lifestyles. It could also be that you want to begin exercising, and the first few times, it is fine, but then you get bored and fall back on all your excuses and never succeed. It is the same for all changes, regardless of whether they are at work or at home. Therefore, many people don't succeed with the changes they aim for and get fed up with trying.

Some people have a brain that wakes up later in the afternoon or at night. In Denmark, we call these people "B-people," whereas those who are right awake in the morning are called "A-people." All it indicates is when your brain is up and running. Since most people have a brain functioning in the morning, I will focus on that. And if you have a brain that wakes up later in the day, you can take what I'm sharing and fit it into your rhythm.

Being an "A-person", I find that it is easier to deal with challenging tasks, make good decisions, and have difficult conversations in the morning. Most people are more willing to take responsibility and ask questions when they have System 2 available. At work, it can be brain-smart (if you are an "A-person") to do all the challenging tasks in the morning instead of postponing them to the afternoon when you are tired and can't access your System 2. If you know a meeting will be challenging, schedule it in the morning. In the afternoon, meetings tend to be longer and fewer decisions are made. If you are a B-person, determine your prime time and do the difficult and demanding task then. For some people, it can be in the afternoon, and for others at night. I know of a few companies that allow people to work when and where they wish as long as they attend the meetings they need to and do their work.

I worked with a construction company where the salespeople got a bonus depending on their sales. Their strategy was to call the customers at 5 p.m. and close the deal. It worked really well; many people were too tired to have a clear overview of the agreement, and the salesperson would also let them know that if they didn't sign now, prices could go up, or they might have to push the date for delivery. They played the fear card, and it worked. Their sales were huge. But when I got to work with the company, I saw how the rest of the company suffered with upset customers who didn't feel satisfied. Some thought they had said yes to one kind of wooden floor and got something different; others felt they didn't know all the options before they made a choice. The company was dealing with their emotions. The unhappy customers were lining up, and the company spent so much time adjusting to make them happy. I told them to quit the bonus for the salespeople and make a bonus for everybody instead. The owners didn't want to do that since they were scared that the salespeople would quit. Instead, they ran workshops where I taught them to work together as a team, and even though it was hard, the salespeople admitted in the end that their strategy was only for their benefit, not the company's.

If faced with a challenging situation, we instinctively try to solve it with our System 1. The problem is that System 1 solves challenges in the same way you have always done. It does not provide new solutions or alternatives and is not critical. Therefore, you also get the results you have always gotten. On top of that, you have the emotions. And if you are tired, challenged, or under pressure, you will rely on what feels good.

System 2, however, will require assessment and analysis—it will take longer and be a heavier and more energy-consuming process for you. Therefore, we often choose not to pursue what we deep-down know would be optimal, opting for the quick solution from System 1, which may not be as appropriate, but we hope for the best.

When you are tired after a long day at work, do you open your cookbook and find a recipe you have never tried before, then head off to the supermarket and take your time to find the best ingredients? Happy and excited, you head home and begin to cook. Well, I don't. If I'm tired, I always make the food I have made hundreds of times before with ingredients in the fridge. If I can avoid going shopping, I will. Many people don't go shopping anymore. It is easier to shop online and have the food brought to your house. And even better, they can deliver ready meals you only have to heat. We use our System 2 to develop easy solutions that fit our System 1. And when we are tired or have had a long day at work, we convince ourselves that we deserve something even easier, so we order takeaway or eat out.

If you want to change how you eat (or anything else), read the next chapter. Then, remember to make it easy to make a change. Let's say you want to eat healthier. Make a food plan for the week ahead and prepare it on Sunday morning when you have a surplus of energy. Make sure to write down all the meals, print or find recipes, and make a grocery list. You can also go and buy everything that is possible to buy ahead of time, so you only need to get the fresh food during the week. Make it as easy as possible for you to follow and implement. Whenever you see anything that can make you fall back into the old habits, ask yourself, what can I do to prevent it from happening? For example, if you come up with new meal ideas but don't find any recipes ahead of time, when the day arrives, you're likely to check your food plan, see what you're supposed to cook, but feel too tired to search for a recipe, so you end up grabbing takeaway instead.

When System 1 is activated, it contacts our limbic system and attaches a feeling to our experience. System 1 will also try to get System 2 to confirm that feeling. For example, suppose you have a negative expectation of a meeting where you know the leader will present a new strategy for the department. You will unconsciously ask System 2 to confirm it. Your System 2 will look for things in the meeting that confirm your System 1's negative expectations. Systems 1 and 2 do that in all matters of life to ensure us that we are *right* and perhaps the others are wrong. Confirmation from System 2 justifies our actions or behavior. If you are late to a meeting and feel bad about it, your System 2 will come up with various reasons for being late. It was not your fault—there was traffic, a queue at the elevator, you didn't know where the meeting was held, or no one had told you about it. But when other people are late, and you are upset about it, you believe they are disorganized; they could have left earlier to make sure to be on time or checked their inbox in time. Again, System 1 brings up an emotion, and System 2 looks for ways to confirm it. If you are a parent, you probably remember noticing prams everywhere when you were pregnant. Your System 1 emotions made your System 2 confirm that having a child was a great idea—just look at all those happy parents! And if you saw a child screaming, your System 2 would convince you that you'd have the easiest child in the world. When we go shopping and feel a positive emotion about buying something, our System 2 will also come up with reasons to justify the purchase, reinforcing the emotion. In this way, we manipulate ourselves through our emotions and convince ourselves that those emotions are correct. If we experience something negative, on the other hand, System 2 will try to justify our actions to help us deal with it.

That leads me to the next tricky function the brain has. Let's say you want to have a month where you don't eat sugar. You decide to begin on the first of the month, which happens to be a Wednesday. You have a tough day at work—many complaining customers and long hours because you had to cover for a sick colleague. Finally, you can drop onto your couch and relax. And then you feel this craving for some chocolate. As we learned before, emotions belong to System 1, and System 2 backs it up to make you feel right. You hear yourself saying, *you deserve some chocolate. It's been a long day, and there is chocolate in the kitchen drawer.* (This is your System 2 talking). *You should go and get it.* System 1 gets up and grabs the chocolate. You begin to eat it, and it tastes like heaven. You feel like having more once you have eaten half of the chocolate bar. System 2 replies that *you should eat it all. Then it'll be gone and won't call out for you tomorrow. Also, it's much better to get rid of it all, then it'll be gone, and no one else in the family will notice it. No one leaves half a chocolate bar in the drawer.* You eat the rest of the chocolate, and then you begin to feel a bit stuffed. And right away, your System 2 says, *what did you expect? You deserve that when you can't live up to your agreements.* See how your System 2 responds to the negative emotion?

When you become aware of this, you can consciously get your System 2 to find positive rather than negative things. The positive is not more correct than the negative, but positive solutions will create much more motivation and influence. It is also possible to train the brain to seek out positive and constructive perspectives to move from being a "pessimist" to having a bright outlook on life—and perhaps even on life's challenges.

Life can become very negative if we exclusively engage our System 1 and do not challenge ourselves to gain perspective. We may also attract others who, in the same way, only engage their System 1 and reinforce our assumptions. We automate as much as possible and create apps, systems, and technology that can help us so we don't have to use System 2. Can you find your way without your GPS? Do you remember your children's phone numbers? ChatGPT is the newest invention that will also make us lazier if we don't pay attention. ChatGPT is excellent if you use System 2 to check the information, stay critical. If we don't, AI can be a real threat to reality.

Meditation is one way to develop and train the Neocortex, which deals with System 2. The research by Danish psychologist Erik Hoffmann suggests that when more energy is directed toward the frontal lobes, which are part of the Neocortex, we achieve a heightened sense of awareness. This also gives us more energy, clarity, and increased mental acuity. Erik Hoffmann's research also indicates that individuals who achieve a balance between what is known as the old brain (reptilian brain) and the new brain (Neocortex) tend to have greater empathy and become more humane.

If we only use System 1, nothing will change.

———

Exercise:

- How many hours and minutes do you think you are using System 2 in a day?
- Do you find it easy to learn new things?

Try to rearrange your day so you begin with the complex tasks in the morning (if you are a morning person). Often, we push the problematic tasks until the afternoon and struggle to complete them. Doing them in the morning will be easier, and you will get better results. And then you don't have to use energy thinking about them for the rest of the day. Prioritize the important meetings in the morning and push the meetings where you know what is happening and don't need much brain surplus to manage to the afternoon. See if you can avoid demanding meetings after two p.m., and if you need to have a sensitive conversation with someone, do it in the morning when we are more likely to listen and understand the message. If you need to tell others about a change, do it in the morning, when people are more likely to understand what you are saying and ask the necessary questions. This applies both at work and at home.

14

MAKE IT EASY—MAKE IT ATTRACTIVE

In my work with changes, I have realized that the essence of making a change happen is comprised of two things.

Make it easy and make it attractive.

Make it easy to do and understand, and ensure a positive emotion is connected to the change so it's attractive. If you do that, you are much more likely to succeed with any change in your life.

In your private life, you might want to exercise more. You talk to a group of friends, and before you know it, you have all agreed to sign up for the next half marathon in your city, even though your condition is poor and you haven't been for a run in five years. The next morning, you wake up, and suddenly, it hits you: you should start to train for the half-marathon! You decide that Monday is a great day to start. But when Monday arrives, it's raining, and you don't have any running shoes, so you decide to postpone it. If you were motivated about the agreement, you would probably get yourself organized, but when you check in with yourself, you realize that you hate running and don't know why you went along with the idea.

One of the things to understand about change is that we need to have a positive emotion about the change; otherwise, we have to rely on our willpower to succeed, and most people don't have that much willpower. When you realize you don't feel like running, you should ask yourself: If I want to exercise more, what would I enjoy? Or what would I feel positive about? If you would like to go running, then make it easy. Don't begin with a half-marathon. Ask yourself what would be easy. If you work from home, you might be able to start with a short ten-minute walk during your lunch break twice a week. But again, make sure you know where you will go and how long it will take. Otherwise, you will hear yourself saying, "I should go for a walk. I don't know where to go, and it might also be too time-consuming." You don't want to give yourself any excuses for not going for a walk. If ten minutes twice a week is too much, make it easier. Make it as easy as you need to get started!

When you get started, you will begin to create a habit, moving it from System 2 to System 1. When you have been going for your walk for some time, you might want to expand it a bit. Eventually, you will walk for thirty minutes twice a week. Every time you begin to get bored, or it becomes too easy, take the level up a notch—not too much because then you will fall back into old habits (System 1). After some time, you can combine walking and running, then move entirely to running. Slow but steady, you build up a new habit, and then you might be able to run one mile and then two, and so on.

I travel a lot with my work, and I don't always get to exercise as much as I would like. I am not a huge fan of gyms because I'm always around a lot of people at work, and I like to exercise in my own space. So, I asked myself, what would be easy and attractive for me when exercising? First, the easy part—I'm not keen on riding my bike or running in the winter. By the time I get home, it's dark outside, and here in Denmark, where I live, it also rains a lot during winter. I had to find something I could do indoors. I bought an exercise bike and a multi-gym so I could easily exercise at home. I didn't have to go anywhere and could do it in my own space. Next, make it attractive—I know I'm not the only one with an exercise bike, hand weights, exercise bands, and other things they have bought but never used. So, I placed a big TV in front of my bike and made a deal with myself that I could only watch my favorite series when I exercised. I love to watch great series, and sometimes I forget how long I have been on the bike. Now, exercising is both easy and attractive, and I go to my personal gym three or four times a week.

It can be tough to hold onto our goal when we don't feel positive about a change. There can be changes we are not positive about but have to make, and then the motivation can be survival or keeping one's job. It can also be getting it done so you can move on to something you enjoy. It's much easier to pursue a change that we are motivated about.

In Lisa Lahey's book *Immunity to Change*, she shares an American study in which people with lifestyle diseases participated. They all knew that if they continued their lifestyle, it would be life-threatening. Some had issues due to being overweight, others from smoking or drinking. There were also other reasons for their diseases, but they were all asked: Do you know what to do to limit the side effects of your disease or even improve your condition? They all answered yes.

The next question was: Will you do it? Seventy percent said no. Why? Because it is easier to continue the lifestyle you are accustomed to than make a change. For some people, knowing you will die if you continue your lifestyle is not enough to change it.

A leader had to make some changes and had difficulty getting the team to follow his directions. His team was grinding concrete stairs, and he wanted the workers to use a new and better machine, and he also wanted them to stand up more. They had terrible work posture, and many of them suffered from back pain. My first response was that two significant changes are one too many. We agreed to begin with one of his goals: Getting the team to use the new machine. I asked him if the team was familiar with the new machine and if they felt confident using it. The answer was no. As they were not confident using the machine, it was much easier to use the old one instead of working out how to use the new one. My next question was, does anyone on the team use the new machine who is happy about it? There was one person. We asked him if he would be willing to show the other team members how it worked and all the benefits of using it. He was happy to share his experience, so we arranged a workshop. The team also got to try the machine, so they became familiar with it. The next step was to make sure there was space in the van to take it to the job site. Something as basic as that can also prevent change. There wasn't space for the new machine since the old one was still in the van. He got them all to swap the machines. A small detail like that could have been enough for the team to fall back into old habits. Now that they had a positive feeling about the machine, and it was easy to take it with them, the change happened. The next step was to make them stand up more during the day. I asked the manager what his ambition was, and he said they should stand up at least ten times a day and do more work standing. How about we begin with standing up once a day? I replied. He looked puzzled and a bit disappointed.

But it is better to build a change slowly and steadily than to succeed for a short time and then let go again.

Many people are way too ambitious about their own ability to make changes. We want to lose ten pounds, run four times a week, stop eating sugar, or work less. And we might succeed once or twice, and then we find an excuse to let go. And excuses are easy to find if you go from not running to running five miles. You will be sore the next day and convince yourself that running is not for you. There is always an occasion or something to celebrate, and if not, we can feel sorry for ourselves, and then we eat or drink the things we are trying not to.

Remember Hannah, whom I told you about at the beginning of the book? When she heard about Systems 1 and 2, she worked out how to permanently change her lifestyle and is now enjoying life. Now, it's your turn.

I hope you get the pattern and can apply it to your life situations. Whenever we want to change anything, we need to pay attention to how we convince ourselves to do or not do something. And if it is too easy to fall back into the old routines, we are likely to do so. You can help prevent yourself from falling into old routines by making it harder to do so. If you don't want to eat sweets, don't buy them. Then you have to get up from the couch and go to the shop to get the sweets; you made it hard for yourself.

The best way to plan a change, no matter if it's at work or at home, is to follow these simple steps:

1. Define the change. I want to...
2. Why? What positive emotions do you have around succeeding with the change?
3. How can you make it easy—to do and understand?
4. When will you start?
5. What do you need to get started? Be specific and write it down.
6. Will you need others, and what will their role be?
7. If you don't get started or are about to give up, look at what you are doing and ask yourself, can I break it into smaller steps to make it easier?
8. If you are working with someone else and they don't buy in on the change, break it down and make it more attractive and easier.
9. Celebrate intermediary goals to keep the motivation and let the brain know you can do it.
10. Be persistent and step into your new identity.

Let's do an example:

1. I want to lose five pounds.
2. Why? I will feel much better, and I'm sick of how I look.
3. The first thing I will do is to stop eating white bread.
4. I will begin on Monday.
5. I need a healthy alternative to white bread. I will make healthy crackers (print the recipe and make sure I have all the ingredients). I will make a portion on Sunday, so I'm ahead and can support myself on Monday.
6. I will tell my family and hope they will support me and not buy white bread.

7. If it's too hard, I will allow myself to eat bread at work and stop eating it at home.
8. I will do this myself.
9. When I succeed, I will allow myself to buy a book I want or something else I will enjoy. I will also begin to manifest; I don't eat white bread if people offer it to me. In that way, I will step into my new identity.

When making changes at work in the form of behavior, the description of how it should be done must be so precise that there's no room for misunderstanding. If the process is broadly described, such as "We want greater customer satisfaction, and going forward, everyone should provide better customer service," employees will use their System 1 to interpret what "better customer service" entails. Had the phrasing been: "We want greater customer satisfaction, which we'll achieve by having all employees greet every customer they encounter in the store with a smile," this would initiate a specific behavior change, and everyone would know how to do it. You can use the same strategy at home when you want to make changes as described above.

PART V

Understanding your Survival Strategy and Triggers
What is really happening?

15

THE ROOT CAUSE OF REACTIONS

When we are challenged, we believe we react according to the situation, but often, our reaction has nothing to do with the current situation. The situation has triggered something deeper in our brain, which is the real reason for our reaction.

According to Dr. David Rock's SCARF model, we have five fundamental domains that we unconsciously guard. His research found that these needs come from primary brain areas that feel threatened if they are not in place. The five domains are status, certainty, autonomy, relatedness, and fairness. If we feel that these areas are looked after and safe, we are able to communicate, cooperate, and feel motivated. When one of them is threatened, we react. However, we are usually not aware of the reason we react the way we do and the underlying drivers in the brain. These five basic human needs are crucial to feel safe and secure. When autonomy is there, we gain freedom of speech and feel freer to do what we feel is right. In my work, I have found that people find it more relatable when I use the word freedom rather than autonomy—freedom in their lives, work, and choices. Freedom is something many people relate to in their everyday lives. When I go through the model, I will use the word freedom, but remember that it is rooted in autonomy. I have also changed relatedness to relationships since it is one aspect of related-ness. In our families and teams, a strong relationship is essential to thrive and feel safe. When we look to the future, building strong relationships will be crucial to creating thriving teams.

When treated with respect, we feel fine and can both listen and communicate properly. We will react if we are not treated respectfully and someone challenges our status. If we can predict the future, we find it easier to manage change and have a sense of security. But if we are not sure what will happen and don't feel that we have enough information about changes at work, we will experience a lack of certainty, which can be very stressful. When we have the freedom to do what we like and solve a task in the way we think is most appropri-ate, we thrive. However, we react negatively if we feel someone is watching us and interfering with our actions. We feel secure when we belong to a family, team, or community. And when we can trust other people, we can be the best version of ourselves. But if the trust is broken or we feel isolated, we can feel insecure and lonely. We can relax if we feel we are treated fairly and there is an openness around decisions. But if we are treated unfairly or others are treated unfairly, we get upset. These are the fundamental human needs, and becoming aware of them can help us understand why we react as we do in certain situations. Then, we can gain the freedom to react more appropriately. Becoming aware of these five triggers also supports our ability to use our buffer zone and make the most appropriate decisions.

In my work, I often coach leaders and work with teams. The first thing I always do is work out which parameters are under attack.

Because if they weren't under attack, there wouldn't be an issue. People often tell me about the symptoms, but I look for the cause. The same goes when you argue with your partner or friend. See if you can work out what it is really about. If you don't get to the source of the matter, the issue will return in different disguises repeatedly.

We all have all five triggers in our brains, but some people don't react equally to all of them. For most people, two to three are more active. Therefore, asking yourself which ones you react to can be good. I react strongly to freedom and fairness. I hate when my freedom is restrained. But I have to take responsibility for my freedom and not blame others. Let's say I overbook my calendar, and a customer calls to check if I can help them. If I scold the customer for calling and tell them they must call much earlier to make a booking, I will project my imbalance on them. I have to point the arrow toward myself and ensure I have the time I need for my lectures and time at the office, as well as time to talk to new customers. If I don't, my customers will trigger my need for freedom because I haven't taken responsibility for arranging my life as I want and need to function. Fairness is so important to me. When I experience unfairness, my brain is triggered. I have learned to pick my battles; otherwise, I will be too busy trying to create a fair world, which is too much to put on any one person's shoulders. (Even though many of us do it). I have decided I won't take responsibility for grown-ups who experience unfairness—they must learn to deal with their issues. If I take responsibility for them, they won't learn anything from the situation. Children are different, so I will help as much as I can. They don't have the resources to stand up for themselves yet. I meet many people who are also triggered by unfairness, and if you are not aware of this and pick your battles, all the unfairness you see can overwhelm you.

Remember, we usually thrive and feel motivated when the five needs are met. When they are under attack, we are triggered and typically react inappropriately.

The Brain's Threat System.

- Status: Being perceived as significant/feeling important to others/social status
- Certainty: Predicting the future (permanent job, tasks, etc.)
- Freedom to decide for yourself.
- Relationship: Social connections, feeling a sense of belonging, trust
- Fairness: Feeling fairly treated.

Status

Status aims directly at our self-worth. How valuable am I compared to you? If you have low self-esteem, you will most likely feel that you are not as good as others or that your opinion is not as valuable as others. This can result in holding yourself back in conversations with others or an inner dialogue where you are critical about yourself.

Do you often think that others know better or have more personal power? Do you talk yourself or your efforts down? Or do you compare yourself a lot with others? Social media is all about how many followers you have and the likes you get. The more likes, the higher the status, and we like to make our lives look amazing online to get a higher status. But for some people, this status is hollow. A young Danish guy bought likes on Facebook and Instagram for a long time. His friends looked up to him and thought he was really something. But then one of the friends discovered that it was all fake. His status disappeared in an instant.

Our status should come from within, not from titles, money, or online performance. But it can be hard, especially if we compare ourselves with others and focus more on what others have and do instead of our worth and wisdom. We can have a high status at the local soccer club, but we might be new at work, and it takes time to build your status.

If someone overrules your decision, your status can be threatened— or if someone changes a decision you made without telling you. It can trigger a string of emotions you might not be aware of, and it's easy to project your reason for reacting onto the other person or task instead of looking at yourself and finding out why you reacted so strongly. Let's say you said no to a sleepover for your child, and your partner changes it without telling you. You lose status and authority. The next time your child wants something, and you say no, there is a way to overrule that: ask the other parent.

It's the same at work. If you make a decision a customer is not happy with, and they call your manager, and that manager gives in and lets them have what they want because he fears losing them as customers, you lose authority. The next time you say no, it holds no power. You can also experience that you make a suggestion at a meeting, but no one listens. Five minutes later, a colleague makes nearly the same suggestion, and now everybody loves it. Then, you need to look at your status and begin to position yourself so you gain respect and people listen. Often, when people don't respect you, they will also overstep your boundaries, which is a sign of them believing their status is higher than yours and they can treat you how they want.

Some people use the way they dress to send a signal of high status, but it doesn't mean that the person actually has high status. Inside, they can be insecure and struggle with low self-esteem, and dressing up can be a way of protecting themselves and trying to gain high status around other people.

A big parcel company planned to open a shop-in-shop in a big department store. The employee in charge had the title of manager, and he arranged a meeting with the CEO of the department store. When he arrived, the CEO looked puzzled and asked where the CEO of the parcel company was. He explained that he wouldn't join them since he had nothing to do with the shop-in-shop contracts. The CEO looked him straight in the eye and said, "I only talk to CEOs, not managers. I have so many managers here—floor managers and this and that manager. Bring your CEO, and then we can talk." The meeting ended, and he returned to his CEO and told him what happened. They arranged a new meeting for his CEO to attend. But since he didn't know anything about the case, all he did was sit there. The manager dealt with the rest.

The other day, I held a course at a harbor, and the team leaders told me that they had been in a meeting with their direct reports, and the CEO had asked if he could join. He would just be there to listen and observe, just to feel the situation in the department. They agreed, which seemed like a great idea at the time. When the meeting was nearly over, the CEO stood up and said, "If there is anything you are unhappy with, just let me know, and I will fix it." The team leader was shocked. First, they knew he wouldn't fix it, and second, they knew that if they told the workers 'no', the workers would head over to the CEO's office and tell him. I told them their CEO was acting like Santa, just swinging by once a year, handing out gifts, and leaving all the mess for someone else to fix. The workers thought it was great, and the CEO got popular. They also told me that the workers often went to the CEO's office to complain, and then he would make changes they didn't know about. This is the worst kind of leadership. It is top-down and full of management by fear. It often results in many people resigning, stress, and replacement of team leaders and managers who dare to speak up. It also creates leaders who are frustrated without status and authority. This was exactly the case.

If you feel you have been overruled or that people don't respect what you say, the best thing to do is talk to the person who changed your decision and let them know how it affects you. Tell them next time you would like them to speak to you before changing a decision you made. That is the respectful thing to do. The challenge at the harbor was that they all knew if they confronted the CEO, he would fire them. Then you must ask yourself if it's worth working in a place like that. We always have a choice; we can quit.

Unconsciously, we scan a room to see who has the highest status when we enter. It can be challenging if you are surrounded by people you believe have a higher status than you. Then, you work overtime to position yourself. Historically, there has been a lot of status in race and gender. To be honest, for some people, there still is. Some white people still think they are worth more than black people. That is a disgrace. It tells me there is a long way to go for everyone to rise to the same level of awareness. The same goes with gender. Let's say you need to get your car fixed. In the garage, there is a male and female mechanic. You talk to the woman and disagree with her conclusion about your vehicle. Do you believe her, or do you turn to the male mechanic? There are still countries where men decide that women can't go to school or must dress a certain way. But I know that many women also feel that, in some areas, men are more valuable than women. In the world, there are more male CEOs, board members, and men's clubs than women. And men have a stronger say in many business areas than women. At the same time, women still have a stronger say at home. I know it can vary, but looking at the big picture, we still have a long way to go before the collective consciousness rises and the status of men and women becomes equal. There is still much work to do to equal race and gender in our world. We all need to take responsibility and make the world a better place for our children to grow up in.

Certainty

The ability to predict what will happen gives us a feeling of being in control and inner peace. If we cannot predict the future, we will feel uncertain and react negatively most of the time. Therefore, paying attention to the level of information you receive when experiencing a change is essential.

Not being able to predict the future is the one thing that stresses the brain the most. It's like driving in the mist. Imagine you are driving on the highway and can't see more than a few feet ahead. You tighten the grip around the steering wheel and lean forward a bit to see better, but it doesn't make a difference. Not until you can see the taillight from another car can you relax, (not the headlight, because then something is really wrong). Now, you can predict the distance to the other vehicle without driving into the unknown. Your brain relaxes again. If we cannot predict the future and feel uncertain at home or at work, the brain is stressed. The best way to deal with uncertainty is to ask yourself, what do I need to feel safer in the situation? I often find that information is a great help. And if you can't get the information you need, ask when you can get more information. If you still feel stressed, shift your focus to what you know. That will help you return to the present. You can also try to feel which emotions are present and embrace them instead of shutting down or jumping into fear.

During Covid, the whole world was screaming for certainty at the same time. When will there be a vaccine? When can we travel again? When can we visit our loved ones? Now, we are asking, when will the war in Ukraine end? And the violence in the Middle East? And what will happen to the economy and inflation? After having years of stability in the world, we experience a lot of uncertainty, and we all must learn to live with it.

In companies I work with, I often experience managers who have worked on a change for a long time and must present it to their colleagues. However, when communicating it to the employees, they leave out details and talk more on a strategic level than on a level that includes the daily issues the team is facing. They take a lot of things for granted because they know, but the people hearing about the change for the first time don't have the same knowledge or experience.

If you are ill and need to go to the hospital, the doctor might tell you what you can and cannot eat and how many pills to take. But when you leave the hospital, your mind is a blank, and you cannot remember what you were told. You are more focused on coping and worrying about what to eat for the next few days when you are not able to go shopping. The information the doctor gave is lost in a haze.

The more we experience change, the easier it becomes to predict our reactions, but we also gain confidence that we can handle it. Therefore, for most people, changes become easier with experience. A department in a university was moving locations, and it was the fourth time in two years. One of the staff told me that everybody was so negative and stressed out the first time they had to move. Their work performance decreased, and more people began working from home. It took six months before they returned to their original performance level. Then, another change happened at the university, and they had to move to another new location. People were negative, complaining that they only just settled and asked where they would move this time. Yet this wasn't the last time they were asked to move locations. But the third time, a change happened in their approach. They now knew the drill, and they could rely on former experience where they, after all, discovered that the new location was fine, and they settled quickly. It went smoothly, and the fourth time, people just smiled and said, "Again? Let's do it."

In a work context, people are stressed about where and who they will sit next to. Is there parking or access to public transportation? Companies are also cutting down on workstations since many people work from home. That opens another uncertainty. Will there be a workstation for me if I go to work? And who will be at work? Will I be the only one at the office? It's also possible that there are not enough workstations for the number of employees, so you have to play musical chairs every morning.

At home, you can feel the uncertainty in many different situations: If you have a date and the other person doesn't turn up, or you get an email from the bank where they ask for a meeting without telling you why. You can also experience uncertainty toward your children, which can be hard to deal with since it can activate many different emotions. Will they thrive at school? Will they make it to university? Are they able to find friends? Do you have money to pay for their education? There are so many things in life we cannot predict; therefore, it is essential to learn to stay calm and grounded even though you are surrounded by uncertainty. Knowing the root of your reaction can help you find out what you need in the situation and help you deal with the challenge.

Freedom

We all need the freedom to make decisions in our lives and the freedom of speech. But not all people have it or can take it for granted. Our freedom can be limited when we sign a contract for a job or a lease. For some people, freedom is crucial in all areas of life, and their quality of life drops if they don't have it. If we demand a great deal of freedom, we can find it hard to be in a relationship, have a permanent job, or even buy a house. The thought of others telling you what to do or where to be at a particular time can feel restraining. And the risk of not being able to sell your house if you suddenly want a change can stop you from buying a home, preferring a short lease instead. We are different and react differently to the five brain threats. It can be hard to understand someone who is allergic to surveillance and micromanagement if you don't care.

You can feel trapped in a relationship where you think the other person is watching you or maybe tracking your whereabouts on the phone. It can feel so restrictive that you will do anything to get some "me" time. People sometimes pretend they are working and use it as an excuse to get some personal space and freedom, or they go for walks with a dog that has already been out for a walk. It's important if you react to freedom that you are aware of how much freedom you need and take responsibility. You also need to tell your family so they don't interpret your behavior as a rejection.

If "freedom" is one of your parameters, pay attention to how you react if the boundaries become too tight in your life or if you have too many appointments on your calendar. Do you react negatively if your manager controls you or you feel you don't have enough influence on your tasks? Many self-employed individuals react if they don't have freedom, which is one of the reasons they choose to run their own businesses. And many people who dream of running their own business want to do it for greater freedom. How we look at freedom can vary from one person to another. Being self-employed is important to me; I don't think I would thrive in a permanent position. I remember when I was employed at TV2, I had this inner drive to gain more and more freedom. But no matter how high I got in the hierarchy, someone was always above me. Even if I became CEO, I would have to refer to a board. So, I became my own boss. That is freedom to me. But there can also be a great deal of freedom in knowing that you get paid every month and you can leave at a particular time and don't have to think about work until the next morning. Knowing you have a job can give you freedom, instead of not knowing when the next customer will call you. There is no one correct way of defining freedom; it can be different for all of us.

If you also have freedom as one of your core values, you must pay extra attention. Then you have a double-up on freedom; it will most likely be very important to you, and you can easily get challenged if you don't have the freedom you need. If freedom is what gets triggered inside you, then that is where you need to focus and work out what triggers it.

Relationships

We all need to feel that we belong. It can be in a team, a family, a society, or as a member of a club. The human brain knows the best way to survive is to be a part of the flock. Therefore, we are also challenged if our flock changes, and it doesn't have to be a negative change. Having a new family member can change your family dynamic and your identity. It can change your routines and affect your freedom. A new team member can be great, especially if you are overloaded with work, but it also changes the group dynamic. For a family or team to thrive, we need trust. Trust is the foundation of a relationship. We can't open up and create the best results together if we don't trust each other. The same goes for friends and family. We need to be able to trust each other. Trust is such a fragile ability, like a thread. You can easily break it. At the same time, fear is more like a thick rope that is far more resistant.

If your brain reacts to the relationship threat, you will find belonging to a group of people is essential. If you work from home, having family or close friends is even more important so you don't feel isolated. It is much harder to create a real relationship when we only meet online. And if you are to start a new job, it is also hard since it can take time before you meet your colleagues in person. Creating a safe and trustworthy connection is much harder online, and it takes a lot of work and awareness. Since many people work from home, we must pay attention to the relationship shift. If we are unaware, we can isolate and build a wall around ourselves where we focus more on survival than functioning in a group or society. We risk shutting down emotionally or becoming depressed and isolated. A consequence can be that we don't share how we feel or lose the ability to make solid and authentic relationships with others.

I always encourage the companies I work with to make it mandatory that the employees meet regularly. I know this is not always popular since it is easier to work from home. But even though we can meet on Teams or Zoom, it is not the same. Our mirror neurons don't work when we transmit through a camera; therefore, we can't connect in the same way. When we meet in person, we create a stronger relationship and can have spontaneous conversations. The relationships we build in person will help us reach out to each other and shorten the distance between us when we work from home.

Privately, many people experience the feeling of not belonging during the festive season or at the new year—if you don't have anyone to celebrate Christmas with or a group of friends to be with on New Year's Eve. Since I have made many changes in my life and lived in many different places, I only have a few very close friends. When I was young, we didn't have social media or a cell phone to help us stay connected. And since I made friends all over the world but never stayed in one place for long, I lost contact with many good friends. Sometimes, that makes me sad, but I know it is a condition I must live with. I also tell myself that it has nothing to do with me personally but is a result of my lifestyle and many changes in relationships and work. So, I make sure to honor the friends I have. Today, there are more young people in the world who feel lonely or depressed than ever before. Therefore, it is crucial that we pay attention to meeting in person and creating strong and healthy relationship bonds.

Fairness

Fairness triggers the brain since we all want to be treated fairly and equally. But many times, it doesn't happen. Races are treated differently, and people from different backgrounds are treated differently.

People with the same skills at work aren't paid the same, nor are men and women in the same job. When we are treated unfairly, we often react with strong emotions, and they can be hard to let go of. If a student of mine evaluates a lecture unfairly, it can take me days to get over. I try my best to let it go, but it's so hard because it's rooted in unfairness. I know that my teaching is always at a very high standard, and I do everything I can to ensure that everybody leaves the lecture with great tools and insights. But I can't make people take responsibility for their learning. Some students believe they are the only ones in the course and must comment on everything I say or constantly ask questions. I always have a choice of how much space I allow them, but it is also a fine line to balance, knowing that if I give them too much speaking time, the rest of the group will be upset, and if I kindly but firmly shoot them down, they will be upset. In both cases, I can get a poor evaluation. When I feel unfairness, I always ask myself, could I have done something differently? What is my part in it? I try to learn from the situation, and if I honestly can tell myself there was nothing I could have done differently, I try to let it go and shift focus to the people who were happy about the lecture.

It is so hard to deal with unfairness because it can activate the emotion of powerlessness. Very often, there is nothing we can do about the situation. It's out of our hands. You can't interfere with your colleague's contracts, the speeding ticket won't be canceled even though you drive ideally 99% of the time, and if you buy a piece of clothing only to find out that the next day it's on sale, there is nothing you can do if the shop doesn't care. If fairness is one of your significant triggers, you will react emotionally. If we can speak up about the things we find unfair, that can be a good thing to do. But we must ask ourselves, is this my battle, or am I fighting another person's battle? I believe that we should fight for children, animals, and nature since they don't have a voice of their own. When it comes to other adults, I'm always a bit more cautious since we can remove their opportunity for learning if we pick up their fight. Let's say you are unhappy at work and find that your leader is not acknowledging your talent and is giving all the great tasks to someone else—maybe someone he also plays pickleball with after work. You tell me, and I can feel how unfair it is. I know you are a bit insecure and don't dare to tell the leader, but I do, and I get triggered by the unfairness and bring it up in a meeting with the leader. Now, I have taken away the opportunity for you to learn to speak up and set boundaries. Always pick your fights wisely, and don't blind yourself by convincing yourself that you are helping the other person—you're not in the long term.

We can all be triggered in all five areas, but notice which ones are more active for you.

Let's see if you can work out the cause of the reactions of the people in a team I worked with. It was a development team in a big international company that had to make a whole new IT platform. They wanted this system to be the foundation of all their systems. There were seven techies in the teams—engineers between the ages of twenty-five and sixty, all with different backgrounds and experiences. One thing they all had in common was that they were at the top of their game. When I was invited to work with the team, they were stuck. The team wasn't delivering the software that the rest of the company was waiting for. It wasn't because they hadn't developed anything, but the process was somehow stuck. I asked them to tell me about their workflow. They said the developers needed to hand over their software to the tester, and the test person would then look for errors, but they never handed over anything. The test people were frustrated and complaining, and the pressure grew from the rest of the company. But it didn't matter; the developers didn't finish their programming.

If you were to help solve this issue and restore a healthy workflow. Where would you look? On the surface, it seems they were a little slow; maybe they didn't take responsibility or weren't talented enough. My focus was somewhere else, trying to find the cause of the issue. I noticed they didn't want to hand over their work to someone else who had to look for errors, so I asked them how they felt about making mistakes. Not many people like making mistakes, and they didn't either. Making mistakes can activate the brain threat system since you lose... *status*. Now, we could get to the essence of their challenge: they feared making a mistake, as it would make them feel and look less qualified. They would lose their status. So, instead of handing over their work and risking a status loss, they held onto it. After we talked it through, we all agreed that making a mistake is acceptable and even better if a colleague finds it rather than the end user. They could move on, and the workflow came back. Bringing awareness into the matter meant they could talk openly about it, and everybody agreed that the end product would be much better if they used each other's skills instead of fearing each other and the status in the team.

Let's look at another example. A ministry had to move out of the center of Copenhagen (the capital of Denmark) to a smaller town one hour away. When I went there, I noticed their great office building and mentioned it. The answer I got wasn't positive. They were unhappy about the place—especially the location, which was one hour away from the city. They thought the former office was much better. I didn't get it; this was new, much easier to get to, and there was even free parking. In the middle of Copenhagen, it's a nightmare to park, and it can take hours to get there in the morning traffic. Still, they were upset. Later that day, we touched on the subject again, and I was puzzled, so I started to dig a bit more to find out the real cause. A year before, the Danish government had decided that many ministries had to move out of Copenhagen and relocate all over

Denmark to make them closer to the Danish people and not be centered in the capital. The Ministry of Employment was one of them. I asked them why they were so upset, and the answer came instantly: A smaller ministry than theirs didn't have to move. They got to stay in Copenhagen. I couldn't help but smile and ask if they ever talked about how unfair that was. They looked surprised and shook their heads. They had only complained about it. When we began to talk about how they felt, they could let go of the feeling and accept the situation. But they couldn't let it go until then because they didn't know what to let go of. I see that often; when we pinpoint the real cause, it is easier to let go. You can relate to the real cause and make a real transformation. It is hard to let go when we complain about the symptoms since our emotions are still stuck, and you haven't fallen through the layers and found the real reason for your reaction. As you can see, when one of the five needs is not in place, we react negatively, and numerous situations can trigger a reaction based on the five needs. If we only look at the trigger, letting it go or learning from it can be hard. It will often lead to an inner or outer conflict.

Working with Your Triggers

With the five brain triggers, it's important to understand that the aim is not to make them disappear. They do serve us well when we use them in a constructive way. But if they take over and run our emotions and decisions, it can be hard to be with other people in a good way—and it doesn't matter if it's at home or at work. Use them as an alarm that sends you a signal that something isn't right. The first step is to become aware that you have been triggered in one of the five areas. Then, you try to locate which one is under attack. Then you Pause—Reflect—Zoom out instead of reacting as you usually do. Begin to observe your thoughts and emotions. Then you ask yourself, what will be the best way to respond? When you do this, you get a choice: Do as you always do or do something wiser.

It is also important to see how a change can activate one trigger and start a chain reaction, taking down some other parameters like domino pieces.

When we know our threat parameters, we can more easily remain calm and objective in a situation instead of going into defense mode or reacting aggressively. Understanding our threat patterns gives us an advantage and the opportunity to respond most appropriately in each situation.

It's one thing to be aware of your own reactions, but it can also be helpful to observe where your family members are reacting. It can save you from many conflicts and unnecessary discussions. When we identify with our threat system, it is nearly impossible to solve a conflict or move on. The emotions hold us back and prevent us from thinking clearly. If your partner gets stuck in one of the threats, you don't have to go there as well. It is much better that you stay in a neutral place and support a solution. Let's say your partner feels unfairly treated and is upset about it. If you begin to pour fuel on it, say how unfair you think it is, and talk about all the previous times it has happened, you both lose. Talk about the current situation and work through it. We can't solve all the problems in the world, even though it would be nice.

Exercise:

Look at the five threat parameters and underline the parameters you react to if they are challenged. Remember, we prefer all of them to be respected; when they are, we feel more motivated and safer.

- **Status:** Being perceived as significant/feeling important to others/social status
- **Certainty:** Predicting the future (permanent job, tasks, etc.)
- **Freedom:** Ability to decide for yourself.
- **Relationships:** Social connections, feeling a sense of belonging, trust
- **Fairness:** Feeling fairly treated

Look at one trigger at a time and ask yourself:

1. Look at people or situations that can activate your [status] threat. Is it a person with more authority than you—a leader or CEO? Is it your father, mother, or another family member? Is it in a meeting when you are insecure and believe everyone else is smarter than you? Be curious and see if you can bring light to the situations or people.

2. Be prepared.

When you have located the situations or the people who can activate your threat system [status], then ask yourself what you can do when it happens that will support you in a better way. This must be something easy and accessible. It can't be... go for a run; that is pretty hard to do during a dinner at home or a meeting at work. But you can tell yourself to take a deep breath. Shift focus. Take a break. Ask a question to find out more. Or something else that will make you feel safe again. Remember that the brain believes it is under attack, and when you can make yourself feel safe, it is easier to react positively.

3. Practice.

Now that you know what can trigger your threat system and are prepared, you need to practice. First, become aware that you are triggered, then practice Pause—Reflect—Zoom out. Then, you'll gain the freedom to keep going or do something different and better.

When you have worked through, for example, [status], do the exercise again with certainty, freedom, relationships, and fairness. If there are some of them where you don't feel you are triggered, then you continue to the next. If you aren't triggered by any of the five, I encourage you to reread the chapter.

It is what we cannot predict that stresses the brain the most.

—Sagar Constantin

16

KNOW YOUR SURVIVAL STRATEGY

Now that we know what can trigger our threat system, we can look at other things that play a role inside us when we are challenged. The way we handle fear is closely linked to how we have learned to manage "dangerous" situations in our past. This is referred to as a "survival strategy." These strategies develop early in life and follow us throughout our lives unless we become aware of them and transform them. Consequently, we might experience using the same strategies and methods to cope with "dangerous" situations, regardless of whether we are twenty or seventy years old.

Survival strategies emerge in our early childhood; we use them to get our most basic needs met, such as love, security, and closeness. These strategies accompany us throughout life and are utilized when we find ourselves in pressured situations. The challenge, however, is that it may not always be the most suitable way to handle a situation, as the pattern is based on a young child's ability to react and survive and is not appropriate for an adult with more resources and nuances in life.

"Our survival mechanism will help us survive but keep us from living."

-SC

Your reaction might be to give up and withdraw, agreeing with everything others say or making fun of what was said. You've experienced in the past that this very strategy works, allowing you to "survive" the situation and once again feel like part of the group. However, you're not happy because you do not stand up for yourself in that situation. Consequently, you might blame yourself afterward for not asserting yourself or for shutting off your emotions, preventing you from feeling the pain of being excluded. You unconsciously use this strategy, and the reaction often occurs very quickly. If you don't become aware that this is not beneficial for you, you won't be able to change it. You might continue to fight fear with fear and lose.

People have many different survival strategies. The most common ones include misunderstanding what is said (so you don't have any responsibility), not listening (shutting down completely and not being mentally present), counterattacking and trying to change the decision (through confrontation, trying to prove your worth, but often making it worse), ridiculing the suggestion (to prevent it), or playing the victim (feeling sorry for yourself and denying responsibility).

If you feel threatened in a situation, one of your survival strategies will kick in, and you will behave in a way that you have previously experienced works for you in these situations. For example, you may find that you are excluded from a new task in your team, which activates the feeling of not belonging.

When our threat system is triggered, our survival strategies are activated. It's advantageous to be familiar with your survival mechanisms so you can recognize them and then, in time, react more appropriately. A need can also activate our survival mechanisms. It can be a need to feel safe, belonging, or loved.

Your survival strategies can make you appear resistant to change, even though that may not be what you want. However, your appearance and reaction to change can be experienced as negative because it comes through a survival strategy. You can begin to examine how you react in change situations, and there may be a correlation with other situations where you have been pressured. That way, you can get to know your own survival strategies, and once you know them, in time, you have the option to choose whether they are on or off. It will give you a whole new freedom to become truer to yourself and what you stand for.

We all have survival strategies, but very few are aware of their deep roots and impact on our decisions. As a result, they unconsciously control most of our choices throughout our lives.

Being conflict-averse is a common survival strategy that is also linked to the reptile brain's function of flight. I meet so many people who avoid speaking up, and instead, they carry anger or frustration for years. In our mind, we can fear a conflict, but if we approach others nicely and appreciatively, most people are willing to help sort out the issue or get a common understanding. We might not fully achieve what we want; sometimes, we also have to ask what the best possible solution is—and not the perfect one.

If you don't say anything to the other person, you will leave them hanging in a bad place. How can they change something they don't know exists? Our new neighbor began to park their car across our driveway, making it hard for us to get in and out. We didn't want to say anything and agreed they could tell how hard it was for us to park our cars. Then came winter, and there was a lot of snow and ice on the road, making it even harder. On top of that, some of their friends had lent them another car that was now parked permanently across our driveway. I decided to talk to them, and they were so sorry for the inconvenience they had caused. They didn't know. We shouldn't be on each other's backs constantly, but when you feel irritated by something, it's your responsibility to reach out to the other person. Then, they have an opportunity to do something about it if they wish.

"Conflicts are not bad. It is the way we deal with them that can be inappropriate. "
    -SC

A survival strategy kicks in when a person feels threatened. It can be a great advantage if you can help the person return to their resources and escape what is perceived as a danger zone. It can be a friend, partner, or colleague. There can be several different ways to do this. Firstly, it can be good to find out where the person feels threatened—professionally, socially, or perhaps in terms of self-esteem. Next, in a personal conversation, you can inquire if there is something that the individual needs to discuss. It's vital that trust and confidentiality are built into this conversation; otherwise, the conversation might backfire. Let them know that you ask because you care.

When I was explaining survival strategies at a lecture at a big windmill company, Jack had the biggest "Aha moment." He said, "I'm a product owner, and every time there is a new project, I spend so much time preparing. I sit up at night and all the weekends leading up to the start-up. I want everything to be perfect, and I need to be prepared. My wife is upset because I can't think of anything but the project and don't spend time with my children. I want to, but something inside me drives me to be overly prepared. I can't control it." He paused. "Now, I know why." He paused again and took a deep breath. "When I was nine years old, I was sitting in a classroom, and the teacher asked me a question; I happily answered, and the whole class laughed at me. At that moment, I decided I would never be unprepared at school again. I have just realized that I have expanded that to my whole life." The whole room felt the realization when he said it. Now, he could begin to face his fear and slowly let go of over-preparing. He got back his freedom.

A woman also had a big "Aha moment" in a course when we discussed survival mechanisms. She said, "I was loud and wild as a child. None of the teachers liked me, and I didn't have any friends. We had a new teacher in the fourth grade, and he was strict. I discovered that if I was quiet, he liked me. So, I began not to say anything in class, and I even had friends, too." She sat quietly for a moment. "As a grown-up, I have always wondered why I never say anything in meetings at work. I have a lot of valuable input, but I never say anything." She looked at me and said, "Do you think there is a connection?" I nodded.

Exercise:

Make a list of your survival triggers and how you react to them.

> If someone rejects me...
>
> I withdraw or go quiet.
>
> If I feel I am wrong or make a mistake...
>
> I blame others.
>
> If I feel less worthy compared to others...
>
> I make sure to be overprepared.
>
> If I want to post on social media that...
>
> I compare myself with others and decide not to
>
> I'm starting my own business...
>
> I must be the best at what I do.

Think through situations where you hold back or change your behavior to fit in. What is the trigger? And how do you react? Be curious and come back to this part since it can be hard to find survival triggers in the beginning. But when we start to look for them, they will appear in more places than we thought.

PART VI

Dealing with Change and Challenges
The Toolbox

17

IS CHANGE A (HATE) GIFT?

When a change or challenging situation occurs, it can often be difficult to foresee all the consequences. Our immediate reaction often arises from what we believe we know and what we have experienced before.

An old Chinese proverb says, "Every challenge is a gift you haven't yet unwrapped."

The challenge of difficult times is that we cannot predict how they will change our lives in the long term or what impact they will have. What might seem like a deterioration in the present could later turn out to be enriching and the other way around.

If you are forced to move, you lose a friend, or your health changes for the worse, it can be hard to see the gift. There is a learning in everything we experience in life, and if we are willing to look for it, all challenges have something deeper to offer than just the actual event. In many ways, life will be easier to comprehend. If you must move unwillingly, it is easy to hold onto how great the old place was compared to the new. You will point out everything that isn't as good —everything from the local shops to the neighbors or the interior design. You will lose if you keep focusing on things you can't change. Instead, you can shift your focus and ask, what can I be grateful for? What works here? How can I take responsibility to make it work or make it better?

Acceptance is the key to getting the most from a challenging situation. As long as you don't accept the circumstances, you will fight or shut down.

A friend had a break-in and realized that their insurance didn't cover everything that was stolen since their insurance premium was too low. They hadn't changed or thought about it for years. She was very upset about the break-in, but as she said, there was nothing she could do about it. So, instead, she decided to share her experience in case she could help others pay attention to their insurance premiums and help them not end up in the same situation. After she told me, I checked our premium and had to double it!

I have been divorced twice, which has been my decision both times. It doesn't make it easy or enjoyable. In my case, I had to move on. The relationships I was in were draining my energy and preventing me from growing as a person. Both times, I had to deal with a lot of anger and unbalanced emotions from the other person, and both times, I lost a lot of money. But I learned a lot! And I wouldn't be without that learning. Even though it was hard, and I suffered from PTSD for over a year due to the last divorce, I wouldn't want it any different. It taught me so much about psychopaths, emotions, and survival mechanisms. I used Michelle Obama's phrase during Barrack Obama's election: "When they go low, we go high." That helped me stay true to myself and embrace the challenge.

I know you might have experienced situations where you would say nothing good came from it, but that is not true. If you believe that, you haven't looked closely enough. There is always a lesson with every challenge. And if we are willing to look and become friends with it instead of fighting it, learning will unfold. Sometimes, surrendering to learning can bring more adjustments and mean we must stand up for ourselves and take responsibility. That is the reason some people avoid change.

Emotions can easily take over in difficult times. This is where you must be very conscious. You can't see the whole picture if you are identified with an emotion. You will see the world through that emotion, believing that it is the whole truth. It happens in football games when supporters from each team begin to fight. There is no logical reason. It's emotions! When challenged by a change, you are more likely to react through emotion than reasoning. Remember, emotions are faster than common sense.

Suppose you can identify the positive and constructive elements of the situation and build on them. In that case, you can take more responsibility and have the opportunity to become part of the process rather than just being a spectator.

"Every change is an opening to something new, and your attitude is crucial to how the future will unfold."

-SC

If you can see a change as a development opportunity with potential and view it with curiosity rather than skepticism, unexpected opportunities will often emerge. In every situation, you must try to stay open and curious.

When John was fired, he was devastated and told me he would never find a place to work that was as good. He loved his job and had so many great colleagues. He was sure it was not possible to find anywhere nearly as good. He put a notice on LinkedIn saying he was looking for new opportunities. It didn't take many days before a company reached out to him. He was a bit skeptical since it was his former company's competitor. He agreed to a sit-down and was surprised by their offer and how well-respected he was. They had wanted to reach out to him for a long time but knew he was happy where he was, so they reacted immediately when they saw his post. After a year, he told me that he was so surprised. The new job was so much better. He had more opportunities and more freedom, and he had fun at work every single day. Not in his wildest dreams would he have made the move if he wasn't forced to do so. And he was so happy that it had happened.

You're allowed to be critical of changes, especially those that diminish work quality and joy, but make sure it doesn't weigh you down, leading you to focus solely on what doesn't work or isn't good. If the change worsens your working conditions, and there's nothing you can do about it, you must choose: Do you want to make the best of it and accept it? Will you fight against it even though you know it won't help? Or will you look for another job? If you accept it, you must stop complaining about it. If you choose to fight the change, make an agreement with yourself for how long you will fight. If we continue fighting for years, we will eventually lose ourselves, and the fight will be pointless. If you decide to look for another job, do it as soon as possible so you don't get accustomed to the change and decide to put up with it but still stay angry. Honor your core values so you choose to be true to yourself. Remember, we always have a choice.

"Focus on what you can change for the better, and let go of the fight against what you can't change."

-SC

Being pessimistic about change can easily become a bad habit we're stuck in. We can break the habit ourselves, but it requires a determined effort.

Observe yourself and your thoughts about change. That way, you start to become aware of your thoughts and feelings. When you realize you are negative, see if you can shift your focus and look for opportunities or places where you can take responsibility and influence. Look for things you can be grateful for and remember to accept the emotions that upset you or make you sad. Don't shut them down or pretend they are not there. Embrace and accept them. That is the only way to transform emotions. They are essential, too. It is your choice. Focus on what brings you joy and energy instead of what brings you down. Both can be there, but like a flower, they will grow depending on whether you water them with attention or not.

Exercise:

Describe the latest change you have experienced:

- What have you learned from the change?
- What are you better at now?
- Which emotions did it trigger?
- How can you deal with those emotions next time you experience a change?

18

ARE YOU IN CONTROL?

Changes and challenges rarely come at a convenient time. They can disrupt your daily routine, which you may prefer to have control over as much as possible—like a storm that damages everything in its way and leaves you feeling helpless. You might live an organized life, where you have saved up and are planning for not just the next week but also the years ahead. You like to be on top of events and hate the unexpected.

Being very organized can be an expression of wanting to have control. Control is a desire to know what is happening, how, and when. It can provide calm and predictability in the moment, but it also has a downside. Control often signifies a lack of trust—trust that you can handle unexpected tasks or challenges, trust that you will receive help and support from others, and trust in yourself.

Many people strive for a sense of being in control and overplan things at times. I used to do that as well when I was younger. I never asked for help and always wanted to do everything myself. If something didn't go as planned, I went over it repeatedly to make sure I knew exactly what to do and say if it ever happened again so I wouldn't be caught off-guard. I worked overtime to be ahead of any situation and constantly scanned my surroundings. When I turned thirteen, my mother arranged a surprise party for me. A part of me always wanted a party, and the thought of being the center of attention and celebration was much better than reality. I was surprised, as planned, and I totally froze inside. I lost control and had no inner preparedness to deal with the situation—and I didn't enjoy it. What should have been a joyful event turned out to be a stressful and painful evening for me. It took me years to realize that I was addicted to the feeling of being in control. Underneath all the different layers of defense was a deep fear of being alone and not being good enough, and even deeper of dying if I let go—that I would fall and no one would catch me. That I was completely alone. The fear of death lies at the last layer when we begin to look at our defense mechanisms, but we rarely think that far. The main focus for the brain is survival, and it will do what is needed to survive. When a therapist asked me years later if I trusted other people, the answer was no. At that moment, I knew I had to begin to work on opening my emotions and trust.

Many people are afraid of their emotions and try to control them instead of becoming friends with them. If we shut down our emotions, we are like robots, and all that makes us human disappears. If you learned to shut down your emotions when you were a child, it can be terrifying to begin to open up again. When we try to control life, it is because of a deep fear that we might not even be aware of. But facing the fear can help us let go of the urge to control.

When I went to New York with a friend, she planned everything. She knew exactly where we were going and when. To some extent, that is great; I also like to book tickets ahead, so you don't have to line up for hours. It is always a balance. My friend didn't leave any room for spontaneity, and when we walked around the city, she stared at the map all the time to make sure we were going the right way as she had planned. She didn't see anything and was all worked up. It was impossible to enjoy the walk since we had to stay on track all the time. I stopped, looked at her, and said, "Let's put the map away and go on an adventure. Let's see where we end up if we just follow our gut feeling." She looked frightened, and I couldn't help but laugh. "Hey, we can always grab a cab if we get lost. We might see something we won't find in the tourist guide." And we did. We walked the streets of New York, ended up at a local bar, and had the most amazing time with some locals. She was so amazed by how life guides you if you let it.

Control is an illusion. How can we be in control? We don't know what others will do or how the world can change in a second. Now can be fine, but your life can change forever in a second. A phone call. An email. Just like that, your life can turn upside down. Control can only be there in a glimpse of a moment, and then it's gone. It provides false security and is very energy-consuming to believe that one can control the challenges of everyday life. You need to think ahead and be proactive in anticipating all possible scenarios. People who aim for control invest resources in analyzing things that can happen to determine how they will act. It takes a lot of resources to be in control and also takes away the flow and spontaneity of life. Some form of preparation is always good, as long as you don't believe that by doing so, you can navigate through life and avoid situations that you have no control over.

The false security associated with control means you work overtime and often become overly analytical about yourself and others. It can prevent you from expressing your opinion or enjoying life thoroughly. You may fear not having everything under control or knowing how to handle unexpected situations. Consequently, changes can seem overwhelming because they shake the false security you strive to maintain.

As with everything in life, it's about finding a healthy balance. We need to feel secure with ourselves, who we are, and what we stand for, and have the confidence to handle the tasks and challenges that come our way. Then, we feel more grounded and confident when we can't predict the future.

Control isn't unconditionally bad. It can be good to control one's emotions, especially in professions such as a doctor, nurse, or police officer. The challenge arises if this behavior extends to all tasks and your entire way of living—or you lose your ability to empathize. That would take away creativity, spontaneity, and ultimately profound joy in life. Control over emotions can be appropriate when you don't want to display vulnerability, anger, or pain. However, controlling your emotions in a relationship and never showing vulnerability or compassion will isolate you from others. Brenè Brown says a true connection between two people can only be created when you dare to show vulnerability.

When you control your emotions, you shut off the connection to the limbic system, where our emotions are rooted, and we cannot feel our bodies and emotions. This means that thoughts take over and produce more thoughts, which may not necessarily provide the necessary perspective. Consequently, it could mean missing out on a situation's nuances. With control, there's a risk of lacking empathy and understanding what the other person faces because control shuts down emotions, leading to relying on a survival strategy.

People who tend to want to control often have difficulty feeling their own emotions or real needs. There is a difference between being able to talk about and describe emotions and genuinely being in touch with one's emotions. Therefore, you can end up fooling yourself because you can put emotions into words but not actually feel them. If that is the case, it can be helpful to begin practicing meditation, where you learn to be present and observe your emotions. On a daily basis, it can be beneficial to be aware of your need for control and ask yourself if you can let go a little and then feel the emotion that arises. This way, you can slowly return and restore the connection with your body and emotions.

Control is based on fear, so examining what you fear is relevant. However, it requires delving deeper into yourself and exploring the things that have happened in your life in the past and have shaped you. That takes great courage. You can do this whenever you feel the urge to prepare or make plans, then ask yourself, is this needed, or is it my need for control? Take a deep breath and be as honest as you can. What will happen if you let go a little? What is the worst that can happen? After reflecting, you can make a conscious choice.

If you experience a conflict at home and try to control your way out of it by saying the "right" things, the situation might stay unresolved. Even though you said the "right" things and the conflict was de-escalated, you might still be angry because you didn't express what you truly believe or stand up for yourself. Or because you gave in and didn't stand up for your values, you allowed your boundaries to be crossed because you used your control to handle the situation and bottled up your feelings. Control can cause us to shut down our emotions, preventing us from feeling our boundaries and standing by our needs in a given situation.

Letting go of control means opening up to trust. Trust can be compared to a muscle. It needs training to function. Start practicing trust in harmless situations. It could be asking for help with a minor task, trusting that you will receive it, or perhaps relinquishing control during a staff event and trusting that others will take over in planning. As you gradually train your trust, you can invite more trust into your life and start letting go of control. Relying on trust will make you more grounded, and it will be easy to stand firm when the unexpected happens so you don't lose yourself.

When you practice trust, you will most likely experience that you can't always count on others. It's important not to revert to your control because it didn't work out the first or second time. Keep practicing. Even if you build strong trust in others, they may not always live up to it. That's also a part of life.

Consciousness gives us a choice in the present moment. When you like to control and be ahead of everything, you can practice building trust instead of control through very small exercises in consciousness. For example, if you want to practice showing trust in your partner, make sure to agree on the things where you let go. And when you let go, don't follow up or expect things to be your way; trust that other people's way of doing something is also acceptable. One thing I love when I'm giving lectures is making fun of how we organize a dishwasher. Some people have a particular system, and if plates and glasses are not put precisely as they want them, they redo it. Well, here is a place to begin letting go of control. And if you do, you can't rearrange it or comment on how others do it. You breathe and observe what it does to you.

Remember, in every moment, we have a choice between fear and trust. If it involves other people, remember to make sure they also know what their part is. If you want to let go of controlling everything at home, you need to be specific about the things you want others to take responsibility for. You can't just let go and expect others to step up if you have taken care of everything for years. It is a process, so remember to make it easy and attractive.

———————

Exercise:

- Find one thing where you can begin to let go of control.
- Share it with the people it will impact.
- Find out if anyone else needs to take on a new responsibility.
- Observe the emotions that are triggered.
- Look deeper into the survival mechanisms that kick in and observe them.
- Give yourself time and let go slowly.

19

THE THREE LEVELS OF CHANGE

When we are challenged or in a difficult place, it can be good to address the change that might occur on the right level to deal with it in the best way. There are three fundamental levels of change: the light "renewal," the slightly harder "change," and the life-changing "transformation." Knowing the level of the change makes it easier to be realistic about the time and effort it will take to deal with it.

Renewal

The renewal is often an external change and is relatively easy to relate to and integrate. You have been to the hairdresser and got a new hairstyle, your friends comment on it, and you welcome the attention. After a few days, you and everybody else have gotten used to your new appearance. If you buy a new car and need to get used to driving an electric vehicle instead of a petrol car, it takes some time to adjust, but after a week or two, you don't think about it anymore. Initially, you spend extra energy on the renewal and enjoy the car's new features. The renewal is easy and often a welcome change that gives a lift to your daily life. It's easy to learn, and you can move fairly quickly from System 2 to System 1.

Whether you decide on the renewal or others do, it's not a big deal. You can manage and don't feel threatened by the renewal. Renewal doesn't have a profound impact on emotions. Most people enjoy renewals, especially if they anticipate a positive reaction from others; it's part of the joy of renewal.

Renewal is a light change that brings a bit of sparkle to our daily lives.

Change

Change is more profound and has far more significant consequences for those involved. This is where we deal with situations like changing jobs, moving house, or divorce—changes that greatly impact our lives.

A change requires more time and energy than a renewal. The difference is also that it impacts us both internally and externally. Twenty percent of the impact is usually dealing with the exact change, whereas eighty percent of a change is what happens inside us. If we are moving to another house, a part of it will be the practical things: packing, sorting, moving, and unpacking the boxes. These are all things that take time and need to be done. But you will get there and, in time, get it done. The greatest challenge is your emotions. Saying goodbye to a home where your kids grew up, all the memories, not knowing how it will be in your new house, and the insecurity around new neighbors, traffic, and noise—that is the greatest challenge about the change and the part we forget to take seriously. We often focus on the tangible and underestimate our emotional state. What if we don't thrive in the new place? What if the neighbors play loud music or use their BBQ all day, and the smell enters your house? What if there are issues that don't come to light until you live there and realize there is nothing you can do about it?

When dealing with a change, the internal processing of the change can take months and, for some, perhaps even years, to get through. Some people never get over a divorce or the loss of a dear family member. There's no way for anyone to see what you're struggling with, which can be difficult. You might have told everyone that you've gone through a divorce, but your colleagues won't think about it after a fortnight unless you bring it up yourself. For you, it will affect your energy, work performance, mood, and emotions over the next several months and maybe even years. But it's not something anyone can immediately see, and you will be expected to deliver the same work performance as usual.

Many people tend to bottle up difficult emotions and shut them out instead of processing them. It might seem easier, and then you don't have to feel the pain. You try to move on, but the pain is still there, reminding you of what has happened. Some people begin to eat more, and others drink or take drugs to deal with the pain. But it's still there. And the feeling will begin to determine how you live your life and influence your life in a bad way. You might start to isolate yourself and slowly lose your friends. You might work more from home and devise many excuses to do so, but the pain is beneath them all. Change emotions are highly underrated and can cause much more pain than we realize and acknowledge.

Even if the change occurs in your personal life, it will impact you at work. Having a child will change your life forever and consume a tremendous amount of energy. Not only will the new routines drain your energy, but you must also deal with all the thoughts, emotions, and considerations that come with it—before and after you have a child.

Phases of change in the workplace, such as relocating offices, merging teams, or significant layoffs, all affect employees for an extended period, thereby impacting their performance. It will take time before everyone resumes optimal work performance. Therefore, it's crucial to critically assess the changes initiated since they will invariably influence employees and ultimately impact the bottom line figures directly.

We may tend not to want to mix our work life with our private life, and in many ways, that's fine. However, we can't deny that what happens to us privately also affects us at work, our performance, and vice versa. Therefore, in some cases, it might be a good idea to mention it to our manager. Not because special considerations need to be taken, but if we've gone through a divorce or lost a family member, it can impact our energy and happiness in our daily lives. When we share this, it can also help others understand our situation. In this way, interpretations and unnecessary misunderstandings can be avoided. And you can also get support from others.

If you work as a manager and notice changes in mood or altered behavior in an employee, inquire about it. Too often, we let people mind their own business because we are afraid of overstepping boundaries or interfering. However, in a change process, it can be comforting to talk about it and experience others showing interest and understanding. As a leader, it is your responsibility to support employees, both when they are at their best and when they are under pressure. If you can do that, you become a much better leader.

If you get fired, you may suddenly have to adjust to an entirely new daily routine. Colleagues and the social network are gone, leaving you feeling much more isolated. You must go out and sell yourself, and your identity as an "employee" disappears. Outwardly, you might be able to lift yourself up and tell others that you are "between jobs," but nobody can see that you might be struggling with low self-esteem, a feeling of being let down, or that your pride has been hurt.

In an education program that I run for businesses, the participants do a presentation at the end where they share what they learned and how it influenced their life to participate. One guy told us about his daughter and took us on a heartbreaking journey where he shared how she got sick as a four-year-old. How they struggled with the health system and had to go overseas to seek help, and how she died two years later. We were all in tears, and the silence in the room was intense. He said it was important for him to share, and the program had given him so many tools to deal with his pain; he knew the pain would always be a fellow traveler inside of him, but he was not fighting it anymore. He was walking side by side with the pain, and it was also a part of his identity. Many of his colleagues didn't know any of this, and they were so grateful that he shared it. He also said that they were welcome to ask him anything. He gained so much respect for his honesty and courage to be vulnerable.

How to Manage Change

1. Be honest and open about the change; that way, others can more easily relate to you and show consideration if necessary.

2. Express how you feel. Let other people know what you need, even though you might not want to talk about what's happening and don't want special treatment. It can be hard for others to ask about a personal change; they can be afraid that you'll express emotions they don't know how to deal with.

3. Get help. Colleagues and friends want the best for you, but they may not possess the right skills to help you with the change. Seek professional help, and you won't overload your colleagues or friends with stories and feelings you're stuck in.

Transformation

Few people experience profound transformation. It is often an external circumstance that initiates this profound transformation. It could be a life-threatening experience where we suddenly realize we must follow a calling or an inner driving force. It might be a revelation where we realize we're wasting our lives and need to change course from one day to the next. It can also be an accident, illness, death of a family member, or another impactful experience that forces us to revise the way we are and live.

When we experience a deep transformation in our lives, we become connected to a place within ourselves where we sense a calling for something greater. It might sound religious, but it doesn't have to be in any way.

Few will understand your calling, and many will respond with "It's probably just a phase" and "It will pass." It doesn't. You have tapped into a place within yourself that resonates more deeply than most people understand.

A transformation might lead you to quit your job and drastically change your career. For instance, you might change from being a successful lawyer to teaching mindfulness in India. Or from holding a high-level position in business to leading volunteer work.

A former colleague at the TV station won the prize for the best TV photographer year after year. Then, one day, I saw a post on Facebook where he shared that he had quit his job, sold his house, and purchased an orchard on an island off the coast. I was not the only one in shock. To me, he was *the photographer,* and he had Channel 2 running in his veins. I went through the comments; one person asked, "Michael, what do you know about apples?" He replied, "I know they taste great." After the TV station had cut down on resources for the documentaries he made, and there was no longer time to look for the exceptional shots, the meaning disappeared. He took his life into consideration: was it all worth it? He wanted something more meaningful, and he found it in growing apples.

Reflection:

Name three *renewals* you have experienced within the last month.
1.
2.
3.

How long did it take before you got used to it? Was it something you decided, or did someone else decide?

Then, name a recent *change* you have experienced or are in the middle of.

- Did you decide on the change, or did someone else?
- How do you feel about the change?
- What emotions are present when you think about the change?
- What can you learn from this change?
- What do you need to succeed with the change?
- If you are stuck, what or who can help you?

It is usually easier to deal with a change that you decide for yourself. Changes that other people decide which influences your life are usually much harder to deal with.

Have you experienced a profound *transformation* in your life?

- What triggered it?
- What emotions were present?

- What are you looking for?
- What is meaningful to you?

20

RESISTANCE TO CHANGE

When you experience a change, there can be three different resistance levels. It is important to address the right level to deal with the resistance in the best way.

>Level 1. Rational resistance.
>Level 2. Emotional resistance.
>Level 3. Relational resistance.

If you receive a notice saying that you can't keep cats in your apartment anymore and you have had a cat for fifteen years, it might not make sense, especially if there is no explanation or indication of the reason for the change. A change like this can activate two levels of resistance. On the first level, you don't understand it. Writing back angrily is tempting, but that will do you no good. You don't approve of the change and, therefore, have rational resistance. But you will also react emotionally if you can't keep your cat. A cat can be like a friend and feel like a family member, and you can't just get rid of a family member. That means you must find a new apartment. Then another emotion occurs: you love your apartment and don't want to move. When dealing with a matter like this with poor communication, it is important to ask questions and do it properly. Don't put emotions in it; you can say you are sorry to receive the notice, but don't begin to write angrily or present yourself as a victim; that won't solve the issue. The person who sent the notice most likely has no say in the matter; they are just the messenger. Get them on your side and acknowledge them. Be kind and open to other solutions. You can also ask if there is a problem with the cats or if there have been complaints. Ask curiously and let them know that you would like to understand the decision and would also be interested in a meeting about the issue if possible. Take responsibility and seek influence.

If you are dealing with a change that hits your Level 2, you must be aware of your reaction. We often express our emotions before we think and can influence others with our reactions. Our feelings can get us to write an angry email or even call the landlord's office to scold them. That won't help the situation. Emotions are so much faster than reasoning, and when dealing with changes, we must keep an eye out for our emotional reactions, learn to contain them, and be curious before we react.

One of my students told me after we went through the theory from this book: "I cannot reach people with rationale if their emotions are challenged." I couldn't have said it more precisely.

The last level, three, is quite challenging to deal with but still crucial to be aware of. If you try to reason or talk to someone's emotions, and the fact is that they don't like you, you have to address that matter and nothing else! Be curious as to what it is about you that they don't like. I sometimes find when asking others what they don't like about you,

you will discover that it is not you but your predecessor, and you represent them; therefore, they don't like you. If you don't talk about that and find common ground, it is hard to work together. It can also be that you remind them of someone they don't like, and they are not even aware of it, and unconsciously, they project their resistance onto you.

When you experience a change and feel some resistance to it, see if you can locate the resistance level. Then, you can focus your energy and hopefully deal with it appropriately according to its level.

1. Get the information needed to support or work with change.
2. Talk about how you feel and get support so you can move forward in a good way.
3. Level with the other person. You don't have to love each other, but if possible, you should get to a place where you understand and respect each other.

21

SHIFT FOCUS!

A change can hurt, and when it happens, it can be painful, too. Sometimes, there is nothing you can do about the change; there is no going back or regretting. It has happened whether you like it or not.

If you are returning from the best holiday ever and your flight is canceled, you can choose to focus on the fact that it is annoying and makes your journey longer. You will be late for an appointment the next day and don't have any extra clothes. All that is a fact. Focusing on it will not change it. You have no influence over the situation, and it won't change if you are upset about it or keep talking about it. Instead, you can shift your focus to your circle of influence. There is always something you can do. It might not be optimal or what you wished for, but there is something you can do. You can find out when the next flight is available and where you can rest and buy some clothes. Since you can't do anything about it, you might as well make the best of the situation.

That is the choice we always have. Focusing on what we cannot change will bring us and the people around us down. I meet so many people who love to tell me about things they cannot do anything about. They complain about the weather, traffic, and public transport. They are upset about decisions made by politicians and managers. When I ask them if they ever tried to do anything about it, the answer is always a bunch of excuses. The more we focus on things we can't change, the more miserable we get. Many people like to complain about things they can't change because they will never be held accountable. It is beyond their control, and it can't be changed.

When you experience a change, make sure to find out if it is set in stone or if you can make an impact on it. If you can do nothing, shift your focus to the areas where you can take responsibility, like implementing the change or when and how the change will happen. If you keep fighting the change, you will eventually lose yourself.

James works in a government agency, and he told me he tried repeatedly to make the managers aware of an inefficient workflow, but they weren't listening. I could tell he was upset, and it meant a lot to him. He wanted his workplace to improve, and since it didn't, he thought about getting a job elsewhere. I asked him what he gained from focusing on it all the time. He was puzzled by the question and said, "If I don't, nothing will happen." "You work at a big organization; they don't make changes that fast," I replied. "If you want to get through to them, you must be persistent. That is the key." He looked at me and didn't say anything. "Make a long-term plan and stick to it. Next time you have a meeting with your manager, bring it up. You will most likely get the same answer as before. They will look into it, right?" He nodded. "That's fine. Then you say to your manager, thanks for looking into it. Is it okay to ask how it's going in a month?" It will be hard for the manager to tell him he shouldn't follow up since that would be the same as saying he is not looking into it. "Then you schedule a meeting in a month and name it *follow-up on suggestion about workflow*. You keep doing this for as long as it takes. Maybe you can change it to a three-month interval but stay persistent. In the meantime, you let it go. You are not to complain or discuss it; let it go and focus on the things that are working. If you don't, it will eat you up and impact all your work." He agreed, and when I met him a year later, he was much happier. He told me that he had met with four managers, and they were making progress.

This strategy applies to all long-term changes in your life. Not everything can be changed right now; sometimes, the timing must be right. In the meantime, look for the things that give you positive energy, spend time with people who bring you joy, and prioritize the things that make you happy.

Without Influence:

A decision has been made, and it can't be changed. It is not open for discussion. It can be good to be clear in your communication when a change is mandatory so other people know that it's the case. Remember to inform people why the decision has been made and make it meaningful, not just something you feel. You should also tell others when, how, and what it means. Allow questions. But if they begin to say they disagree or make other suggestions, then hold on to the decision and shift focus to the areas where they have influence.

You might decide it's time to spring clean the house at home. That is compulsory. But your kids will have the opportunity to say which rooms they will clean and when. That is in their circle of influence, and you make that clear. They cannot say that they don't want to do the cleaning.

We often waste so much time and energy discussing something that can't be changed instead of looking into how we can best manage it.

With Influence:

The things in our circle of influence are the things we can change. We can take responsibility for our share of an assignment and engage ourselves in the work. In that way, we focus on positive feelings and thoughts. It doesn't matter if we are at work or at home. We always have to follow some rules. And if we keep fighting other people or the rules, we will waste time and energy. There is always something to learn and something you can influence.

Many of my engagements are in Copenhagen—a four-hour drive from my house. If I complain about it, it will make me feel negative and make me not look forward to the events. If I focus on the distance and why there isn't a bridge that connects the country better, I will waste my energy and time. Instead, I shift my focus and ask myself, if I have to sit in the car for four hours, how can I make the most of it? The answer is listening to audiobooks. I don't have much time to read and would love to read more. In this way, I use the time to do something I long for, and I feel entertained, too. Sometimes, I even look forward to the drive to continue a book.

We can do that in all situations of life. Shift your focus. I also teach it to my twelve-year-old son, who sometimes finds school boring. If classes are boring, focus on the time with your friends. Challenge yourself in every lesson; find one interesting thing. He sometimes gets fed up with my positive attitude, but it works. And I remind him that he is there anyway; he might as well make the most of it.

Remember, if you believe you can change something, go for it. But if it begins to eat you up and you are about to lose yourself, let it go. Shift your focus to what you can influence and find happiness in it.

Exercise:

- Find one thing you can't change that you keep complaining about.
- Then, begin to be curious: how can you shift focus and take responsibility for making the most of it?
- Write down as many things as possible that you can actually do or have influence on.

22

STAGES OF CHANGE

When experiencing a change, there are phases that we all go through. Knowing the different stages and being able to recognize them can help you avoid getting stuck, or if you have friends or coworkers who are stuck, you can help them.

Some people quickly skip several phases, while others need longer in some of the phases. It is important to find out where you become challenged and what it takes to get through the process in the best possible way. When you begin recognizing the stages, it is easier to discuss them and move forward. Knowing the phases can also be helpful so you can express the different stages and, in that way, also help others recognize what is happening.

The change.

The moment the change is presented, the process begins. This can be a small or a big change; it doesn't matter if you decide on the change or if others do. It can also be a situation that changes or a shift in someone's opinion, such as a politician shifting from one party to another.

Denial or shock.

This is usually the first reaction. You try to keep the change at bay and act like it's not real. Denial is often manifested by either blaming others or insisting that it has nothing to do with you. The shock itself can make you unable to feel your emotions. You shut down and act as if nothing is happening, thus also denying it. If you get a life-changing message about your health or family, you can be in denial for quite some time until reality sinks in and you accept that the change is real. It could also be a change at work, where you hear yourself saying: they have talked about this so many times, it won't happen. Or that you get a message from a family member you haven't seen for ages saying that they will come and visit, and straightaway you think, that's not going to happen, just wait and see. And then they do come, and you are likely to move on to the next phase.

When the world began to hear about Covid, most people were in denial. *That is not entering our country*, or *we are too smart to let anything like that spread. China is far away.* Many people held onto denial for a long time, and some even tried to convince others that Covid didn't exist.

In denial, we reject reality and hope it's a bad dream from which we will wake up. Some people will fight to hold onto denial and try to convince others. Even if we realize we are not right, we will cling to our version of the truth so we don't lose face. We often fall through to the next phase when we realize it is happening.

Anger.

The anger can be directed both inward and outward. You can blame yourself for not seeing the change coming, not getting more done, or perhaps missing the opportunities. When the anger goes outward, it's more about how others have failed and whose fault it is. When it's directed toward yourself, you talk yourself down and criticize yourself. Whether the anger is directed inward or outward, handling the change will be challenging if you are in this phase. Many people can stay or return to this phase for an extended period. They can hold a grudge against you, politicians, the government, or God and tell themselves that it is fair to be angry.

You can remain in anger or denial for an extended period, and it's essential to take this seriously, as you will unconsciously work against the change and perhaps project emotions onto others. You can become identified with the battle against the change.

When people realized that Covid would affect our lives, many people got upset. We began to blame the ones that carried it into our country. Here in Denmark, it was brought in by people who went skiing in Austria. And it was also easy to be angry with the government for not closing the borders faster and checking the people crossing borders.

But the disease was here, and there was nothing to do about it, so we fell into the next stage.

Uncertainty.

Uncertainty is one of the hardest things to deal with when a change happens. Not knowing what will happen and being able to control the future stresses the brain the most. There are differences in how well people can cope with uncertainty. Some people need a lot of certainty, while others thrive in the flow of life.

At work, we can be in the phase when there is a layoff, when we get a new CEO or leader and don't know their priorities or if we will get along. At an election, there is a high level of uncertainty both before and after. As I mentioned earlier, uncertainty can create mist in the brain and frighten us. What is happening? Will I be able to cope? How much support will I get? If you prefer to be in control, you will be working overtime in times of uncertainty. It is an excellent time to learn to lean on trust.

When the prime minister in Denmark locked down the country due to Covid, all people were asking for was certainty. And it was the same picture all over the world. *When can we go back to work? When can we get a vaccine? When can we visit our loved ones? When will it go back to normal?* All over the world, people were screaming for answers nobody had. It was the first time ever that people had faced the same challenge all over the world and needed to learn to be in the present and live with uncertainty. Some coped better than others. And if you couldn't cope, you would fall into the next phase, apathy.

Apathy.

Change can seem overwhelming, and you might feel resigned in this phase. Does it all matter? Can you trust what is being said? Everything can seem crushing, and the reaction becomes resignation. You can't change anything anyway, so why try?

Jeffrey works at an international company producing computer chips and told me he was apathetic. He tried to reach out to his manager several times to tell him he was bored and demotivated by the tasks he was doing, but the manager never replied. He was busy attending meetings. He said that he had felt like that for two years. I was shocked and asked, "But why haven't you done something else?" He said he stopped believing it mattered. He came to work, did what he needed to, and went home. We agreed that he should try one more time to set up a meeting with his manager, and if he couldn't get through to him, he had to go higher up in the system. By coincidence, I met him three months later, and he was beaming. The light was back in his eyes, and he was smiling all over his face when he saw me. He managed to get an appointment with his manager; together, they found a new position for him where he could learn new skills and be challenged. He was so happy. He got out of apathy.

Most people had to stay home from one day to the next during Covid. Schools closed, and people weren't allowed to go to work. People who lived alone got lonely, and people who had to work and look after their kids simultaneously got stressed. For many people, it was hard in the beginning, and some gave up and withdrew. In this phase, we don't believe that anything will get better no matter what we do. Some people stayed in their PJs all day; others began eating more unhealthy food, and some lost their motivation. And when we lose our motivation and sense of purpose, we become sad or depressed. If you are in this phase or know people who are, please contact them or ask for help. It can be hard when we lose hope, and a loving push from someone else can make a big difference. When we are ready to move through this phase, we can be struck by sorrow... by the loss the change brings.

Sorrow.

When you are grieving what you are losing, you have reached the bottom of the curve of change. There is a big difference in how much you feel you lose. Some people move on quickly, while others experience the change as a great personal loss. Many people skip through this phase or neglect it. Along with change, there is often a goodbye to someone you know, something that feels good, or something you are good at. It can be a program you use at work, and you just love it, or a game or a series. It can be a great colleague or a leader. It can be a pet or a friend. Other people might not understand your grief, and you can't expect them to. Until I had a cat as an adult, I didn't understand why people were so upset when a pet died. It's hard to put yourself in other people's shoes when you haven't felt what they feel. When we lost our cat some months ago, I was crushed. The house felt so empty, and he had become a family member. I still get really sad when I think about him, and it hit my threat system of unfairness since a car hit him when he was on his way home, one street away from our house. I don't expect others to understand, and it is a grief I carry in my heart. After grieving for some time, you can move on and still carry the sadness. In time, it will heal, and it's easier to embrace all the memories.

During Covid, many people couldn't visit their loved ones; some got stuck in a foreign country for years before they could return, and others were isolated in their homes. People had to go into quarantine, and we weren't allowed to travel. Some people suffered from depression, and many young people got lonely. Relationships and remembering to reach out were more important than ever. A man in one of the companies I work with said that coming back to work after Covid was the best day of his life. He hated being at home without seeing anyone but his wife. He was definitely not retiring any day soon.

In time, we move through the phases if we allow acceptance. It is the key to transformation—not shutting down and not caring. That is not acceptance. Acceptance comes from a deep place in our hearts and is the one thing that truly can help us move on. Acceptance doesn't mean shutting down or forgetting; it simply means accepting things and circumstances as they are—something we must live with and take responsibility for. We let go of the negative emotional strings attached to the situation and look toward the future.

Accept.

In this phase, people begin to surrender to what has happened and no longer focus on what they have lost but on the fact that this is the way it is now. We start to focus on how we can make the best of the situation, and we focus on moving forward.

Acceptance can be really hard, and we can easily fool ourselves into believing we have accepted the change, but when we talk about it, there is still a touch of negativity or bitterness.

I visited an international company that maintains offshore wind turbines. They were so frustrated by some changes, and the moment I entered, I could feel a wall of negativity. Since I listened to them, they also projected all their frustration onto me. They didn't feel anyone took their suggestions seriously, and they had tried for years to get through to the manager. The manager was the nicest person and wanted all the employees to feel good and be happy, but the more he gave them, the more they expected. And since times had changed, he had to raise the bar and ask them to step up. They were not happy at all. He did listen, but their demands were not his to solve; there were things he couldn't influence. I told them that, and one man answered, "Do you want me just to forget it and not care?" That is the problem. He shifted from one side of the pendulum to the other—from wanting something on one side to giving up and not caring on the other. I told him I wanted him to go to the center of the pendulum and accept that just because you want something and make a suggestion, it is not certain you will get it. There are things we cannot influence, and trying to do so can be a waste of energy. In his world, he either fought or gave up; there was no in-between. But if he could begin to accept the change, he could also take responsibility and move to the next phase.

Negotiation.

Now, you start to see the energy emerging to shift the focus from what you lost to what you can achieve. At the same time, there may be a budding engagement and interest in the change. There is a new reality, and within the frame, there are always possibilities. We just need to look for them and begin to take responsibility.

Refocus.

Renewed energy begins to appear, and efforts are made to find "meaning" in the new initiatives. At home, you begin to see all the great things you learned from the change. You begin to adjust and focus on the improvements and what you have rather than what you lost.

Employees find their new roles and positions at work in relation to the changes. If the change has been implemented satisfactorily, employees will begin to look forward and actively participate in innovation and new ideas.

Engagement.

The change has now been implemented, and it gradually becomes the new everyday reality. It may be that the benefits of the change begin to show, and people will now look forward and build on the initiatives that have been made. When you have reached this phase, you can start to enjoy life and have the surplus to manage another change.

We can go through the phases several times in a day, with small and big changes. Let's say you have a special favorite dish you want to make. You go to the grocery shop to buy a specific spice that gives your dish the secret touch. When you get there, you can't find the spice and know this store is the only one selling the brand you like. You look at other shelves and ask staff if it is true, but they don't have it. It must be there somewhere. It's not. You become upset and can't believe they don't have it. If you see the manager, you will tell him they should pull themselves together. Now, you don't know what to have for dinner or if you can ever make your favorite dish again. You might as well not eat anything for dinner or just take something from the freezer, and you will definitely not cook anything. But then you realize that you are also a bit sad that you can't make your favorite dish you had looked forward to. After some time, you come to terms with the fact and begin to wonder if any other store might have the same spice from another manufacturer that would work. Or maybe you could try the dish with a different spice. You head off and go to the store down the road.

In a cooking situation, we go through the phases quickly, and if you are curious, you will find many more situations in your life where you go through the phases. The better we get at recognizing which phase we are in, the easier it will be to move on.

Not everybody goes through the phases; some jump from change to engagement. But most people fall through the stages. We don't always begin in denial; you can start at any other stage and go up and down before you reach acceptance. Some people spend a few minutes in the change curve, others years. There is no right or wrong. If you experience another person being stuck in the change curve, you can support them by asking about the stage you believe they are in and trying to explain what it means. It can be hard to let go when you are unaware of where you are stuck. By expressing the different stages and putting words to what it means, you can help the other person.

———————

Exercise:

- Do you recognize any of the phases?
- Can you think of any changes in your life that have caused you to enter one or more of the stages? What happened, and what did you do to move on?
- Which stage are you most likely to get stuck in, and if you do, how can you support yourself to move on?
- Do you know anybody who is stuck in a phase, and if so, how can you support them?

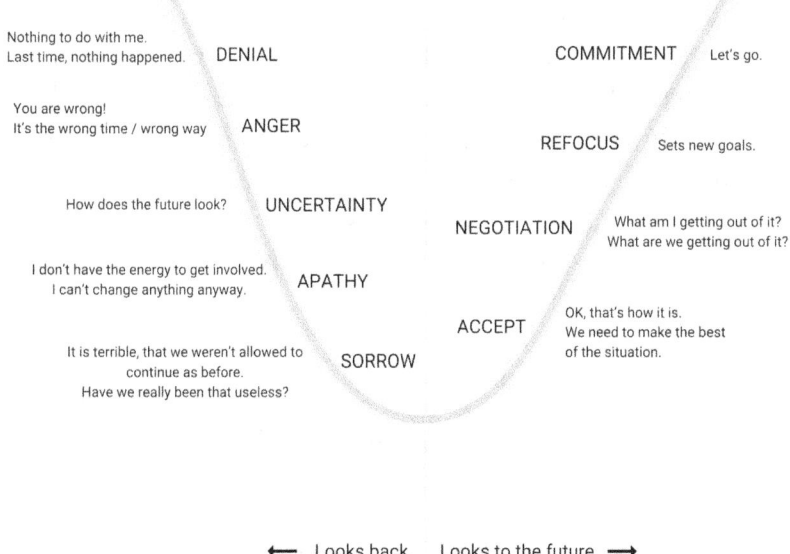

CHANGE

Nothing to do with me.
Last time, nothing happened.   DENIAL

You are wrong!
It's the wrong time / wrong way   ANGER

How does the future look?   UNCERTAINTY

I don't have the energy to get involved.
I can't change anything anyway.   APATHY

It is terrible, that we weren't allowed to
continue as before.   SORROW
Have we really been that useless?

COMMITMENT   Let's go.

REFOCUS   Sets new goals.

NEGOTIATION   What am I getting out of it?
What are we getting out of it?

ACCEPT   OK, that's how it is.
We need to make the best
of the situation.

⟵ Looks back   Looks to the future ⟶

23

KNOW YOUR ABC'S OF PSYCHOLOGY

When we talk to another person, we unconsciously pick up on the tone of voice and body language and mentally complete other people's sentences before they do. We believe we know what they are going to say, and often we don't listen. We rely on what we think they mean even though they say something different. When we read a letter from the council, we only read what we find important and sometimes make up our own reality. We hear fragments of a conversation and believe we know the whole context.

The brain is lazy and will make up its own reality based on previous experiences and what it believes can happen in the future. None of it needs to be true.

That can be a real challenge when we talk to others or try to work together. It can also be a real challenge when you pass on information or get information from other people.

There are three phases.

> A: *Activating event*
> B: *Beliefs*
> C: *Emotion*

A: When there is an action, there is also a reaction. When we communicate with others, we are not always specific and clear in our communication. That can trigger phase B, the interpretation or assumption. It can also be that we look at another person in a certain way, which sends them right into phase B.

In phase A, you are dealing with something in the present moment. It can be a conversation, an interaction between people, or something you see. Here, you pay attention to what you hear, read, or see and reply to that.

B: Depending on the quality of the communication or the situation, you might fall into phase B. If someone tells you something you don't understand or can't relate to, it's easier to interpret than ask a clarifying question. You try to fill in the gaps with what you think the other person means or wants. You do it according to what you have experienced previously or believe. You make up a reality that might not be real. In this phase, you relate to the past or future rather than the present. You draw upon experience from the past or what you think will happen in the future. The other person might try to pass on a message, but your brain makes up a different reality and begins to make its own conclusion based on what you believe to be true.

C: From phase B, we fall right into phase C. Here, we connect an emotion to our made-up reality. The emotion is usually not positive. The emotion makes our belief regarding what you said even stronger. We are still using the past and future as a reference. We are filling in the gaps in your communication with what we are usually told, what typically happens, or what we believe could have happened.

In phases B and C, we pick parts of what is real and make up our own version of reality. This is how we misunderstand each other and where many conflicts begin. The brain is working overtime to look into the future, trying to determine what will happen. It makes up many different scenarios and stories you might consider to be accurate. Racing thoughts and worries come from phases B and C. Phase B contains all the thoughts, and phase C fires them up with emotions so they become stronger and more real.

Making interpretations is not all bad; the brain needs to pick up known facts and connect them with new information all the time. If we had to relearn everything from scratch all the time, the brain would burn out. It is when we are not conscious of the pattern or how we use it that it becomes tricky. We need to question our interpretations to find out if they are valid.

Let's say I ask my son if he wants to go to the shopping mall. I need to return a pair of shoes, buy a birthday gift for a friend, and buy some groceries. He happily comes along, thinking we will go to the gaming shop, get an ice cream, and maybe even go to the movies. The outcome of our trip is easy to predict. If I had said, I'm going to the shopping mall to return a pair of shoes, buy a birthday gift, and get some groceries. Do you want to come? He would be able to relate to what I said and make up his mind based on facts and not his interpretation. His answer would be: no, thanks, I'll stay home. There's no conflict, and there's respect both ways.

When we are unclear in our communication, we leave gaps for others to interpret and risk creating an unnecessary conflict between us that we are not even aware is happening.

To prevent it, ask yourself, can I be even more precise in what I'm saying? If you tell your kids to tidy up their room, you might begin by defining how you think a tidy room looks. If you just say, tidy up your room, there might still be clothes on the floor and dust on the table. If you say, I need you to empty the dishwasher, you have not said when, and you might be upset when you come home from work, and it's not done. But the teenager was going to do it later.

If someone says, I need the answer next week. Well, they might get it Friday at 4 p.m. when they needed it by Wednesday and thought I knew. You can also have a friend who asks you, "What are you doing tomorrow?" You shrug and say nothing. "Great, I'm moving flats and need someone to help me." Or you could ask someone, "Can you help me?" Well, I don't know unless you tell me how you need help.

We are lazy in our communications, and that leaves considerable room for interpretation. We can assume that other people are doing things to upset us, but if we haven't asked or looked into the situation, how can we know? Some people will say that is how they have always been. Well, that is a poor answer; we all change. And we need to allow people to change. At any given moment, something new can happen—a new opportunity. So be curious. If people tell you something that leaves too much room for interpretation, ask them to be more precise.

We can also hear or read something, and our brain will jump right into phase B or C. The situation in the world is constantly changing. Right now, there is a war in Ukraine and a conflict in Gaza. People are afraid. Just the other day, Ursula von der Leyen, President of the European Commission, said: we should prepare for the risk of war. Since then, I have met so many people who jumped right into B and C and have bought canned food and water. My mother even bought a camping stove in case someone hacks the power grid. A comment like that activates fear, and my grandparents lived during the Second World War, so my mother has heard many stories that activated B and C. I'm not saying if it's good or bad, clever or naïve. She could be right and well-prepared, unlike me. For me, it is important to come back to A... what do I know right now? That question will help me relate to the present moment as reality. Now, I can make a conscious choice and not one based on fear and the past.

What do I know right now?

I know that Ursula did make a statement. I know that there is a war in Ukraine. I know that Putin is in power in Russia. That is what I know. If Russia will invade Europe, I don't know. I don't know if the power grid will be hacked. Now, I can make a decision based on what I know. I might think: well, I want to feel safe and prepared, so I will store some food and water. Or it might be that I decide to take it as it comes and trust in humankind.

Asking: *What do I know right now?* Let's look at facts, which will bring us back to the present, where we can make a conscious decision. We can also ask: Is it something I believe, or is it something I know for sure?

If you have children who have reached the age where they begin to go out, you will most likely also have lain awake at night, worrying if they are okay or when they will be home. When you hear the door open, you can finally fall asleep. Until they are home safely, you make up all kinds of scary scenarios. Most of them will never happen. They are just thoughts that keep you awake. When we worry a lot, we also teach the brain to worry. Then, it can be good to stop the thoughts by asking, *what do I know right now?* I know my kid is out with friends, and I know that I raised him well. When he will be home, how much he is drinking, and who he is with—I can't know. I have to let go and trust that I did my part in his upbringing.

My family can all see each other on Apple's "Find." When I asked my son, who is 21, to add us, he looked at me and asked why. Well, I don't care where you are, and I won't use it unless you need to be found. But if something happens and you can't reach out for help, I would like to be able to find you. He looked at me and said, well, I would like to be found, so sure, let's find each other. So far, it has come in handy several times. Once, we were going to the movies, and I was with my younger son and girlfriend at the movies, waiting for my older son. The movie was just about to begin when he came rushing in and said: I thought we were going to the cinema near your house, so I went there but couldn't find you, so I looked at Find and could see you were in the city, so I rushed here. He also looks at Find before calling me to ensure I'm not with a client.

Misinterpretations can quickly become gossip, spreading rapidly in a family or workplace. Before passing on gossip yourself, check with the person what is true and what is false. That way, you ensure you won't be the one starting a wave of false rumors that cause more harm than good. Remember, we all have a responsibility for a relationship and a conversation. You can ask questions if you don't understand what I am saying. Don't leave other people in a bad place where they think everything is fine and you don't.

We make a lot of interpretations every day. See if you can be aware of when you move into B and C, and then ask yourself, what do I know right now? And come back to the present. It can help you if you worry a lot or have too many thoughts all the time and never have a quiet moment in your head. Stop the thought by returning to the present.

24

SETTING HEALTHY BOUNDARIES

Setting healthy boundaries can be helpful when building your inner rock and beginning to stand up for yourself. Some people find it easy to say no, but many are afraid of the conflicts that saying no or setting boundaries can bring.

When we say no to another person, we reject them, and I don't know anybody who enjoys being rejected. Many people don't want to do to others what they don't like themselves. When you don't want another person to feel rejected or inadequate, you choose to compromise with your life rather than hurt others. One could say that is noble, but when you begin to compromise and lose yourself, it's not. A woman told me that her friend, for over fifty years, was constantly overstepping her boundaries. She was so fed up with it that she considered cutting off the friend. I asked her if she found it hard to set boundaries, and she said it was no problem at work, but it was hard to do so with people closer to her. Instead of cutting off her friend, I suggested she use the situation as an opportunity to learn. First, she had to look at her fear. Why didn't she say no to her friend or tell her she shouldn't interfere with her business? She wasn't afraid to lose the friendship, but she was worried it wouldn't work. She tried before, but her friend didn't respect her "no" response. I asked, "Has it always been like this?" She nodded. "I believe you must be very honest and tell her how you feel. Have you ever told her how her way of being makes you feel?" She shook her head. Her friend has a temper, so she was also afraid of her reaction, but I told her, "You can't know how she will react. But remember, you are allowed to walk away anytime if it becomes uncomfortable. And one more thing, she might not be aware of her own behavior and how she is in everyone else's business. It might be a survival mechanism for her." She decided to be honest with her friend, who became very sad to hear how she felt, and they agreed that she would tell her when she was too much from then on.

When you don't set healthy boundaries, other people will begin to disrespect you and take you for granted. Slowly, you will also begin to disrespect yourself and talk yourself down, telling yourself you are not worthy and others are more important than you.

The first thing to become aware of when we want to set healthy boundaries but don't is that fear is holding us back. If there were no fear, we would put our foot down. Often, the fear is unconscious and needs to be addressed to change our approach to others. On top of the fear, we make excuses and avoid dealing with the real issue.

It is usually the other person's reaction that we fear. Will the other person become angry, disappointed, or sad? Will they shut us out of the community, family, or team? It can also be that you don't think you are allowed to say no or have learned that your no doesn't matter, that the other person is more worthy than you.

Before you can set healthy boundaries, you need to address your fear. But you also need to settle your mind about your decision. You can't set a healthy boundary if you are uncertain or vague.

Let's say you don't feel like going to the movies with a friend, but your friend is begging you and telling you how she went with you to a concert even though she didn't like the band. You feel guilty and don't want a conflict, so you give in and go along. If you had stopped and asked yourself, what am I afraid of, the answer might have been: Hurting my friend, that she will miss out on the movie, that she won't go with me in the future, or if we look a little deeper, that your friend will become upset and won't reach out to you again.

We fear the other person's reaction and let go of being true to ourselves.

Another person's reaction can also be: Why are you always so boring? Or angry? Or not nice? Then, we give in and let go of our boundaries. We don't want to be like that. It is a compelling way of getting other people to give in—accusing them of something you know they don't want to be (and they are not!).

Years back, a friend told me that I was very tough to be with when I said no. I looked at her and said, you know I'm not—I'm just very clear in letting you know what I want and don't want.

Another thing that can also make us let go of our decision is the boomerang effect.

The boomerang effect comes into play when you tell your friend that you can't go to the movies, and then your friend says, well, I won't invite you again. BANG. You get a rejection right back. Let's say I have a customer who calls to book me for a conference, and I don't have any available time until after the summer holidays. I tell them I would love to work with them, but it has to be later in the year. If they say, well then, we won't call you again; we need it to be right now. Of course, that would go right to my stomach, and I would feel the fear of missing out. And if I'm not careful, my mind will jump into assuming and begin to make up a reality that is not real. It might say, what if a significant influencer at the event writes about your books? What if there are people who can support you? The fear taps into my dream or hope, and now I'm just about to rearrange my schedule and say no to companies who booked a long time ago—IF I don't see the pattern and stop myself, take a deep breath, look at my fear, and fall back into trust. They used the boomerang to try to get their way and force me to let go of my decision.

When you begin to see the fear of other people's reactions and the boomerang effect, you can move to the next step of setting healthy boundaries—narrowing it down. Setting boundaries happens in your head, so you need to find out what you are telling yourself when you want to say no. When you begin to see that it is the same thing you tell yourself repeatedly, you can begin to stop it.

The next step is to look at what or who you find it hard to say no to. We usually generalize. "I'm bad at saying no." That is not true; you might be bad at it when it comes to your father or boss, but you can say no to your friends and kids. Or perhaps you tell yourself you can't set boundaries at work. Not true. Is there a colleague who challenges you? Is it at a meeting with people you know or people you don't know? Does it have to do with tasks? It's not all situations at work where you can't set healthy boundaries.

We should always use time, tasks, or skills at work when we say no. "I would love to help you, but I don't have time today." Or "I would be happy to look into it, but it's not my area of expertise." It is not the person I say no to; I acknowledge them, but I use time, tasks, or skills to say no. If they push, I will say: If you insist that I help you today, then we need to agree on what other task can wait. Look at the priority.

Sometimes, we don't set boundaries because we don't want to cause a situation, or we might think that others will like us more if we are pleasers. You can also convince yourself that it will pass, so why make such a big fuss about it? Unfortunately, it can build up like the woman and her friend for fifty years. It usually doesn't disappear; we either shut down and ignore it or do something about it. So, when you notice irritation building, pay attention; it is much easier to do something about it before it becomes a big problem.

It can also be unpopular to say no. I even meet people who say they are not allowed to say no at work. That creates a dysfunctional workplace where people are not safe and don't thrive or succeed at the level that is possible.

Setting boundaries can be hard if you are tempted by the offer, but know it's better to say no thank you. Let's say someone offers you a new job. You love the people where you are, and you are happy. But you are also flattered by the offer and don't want to disappoint them or have them think you are not grateful. You become vague in your response. Now, it's easier to make you change your mind or let go of your boundaries. If others sense an opening, they will go for it to fulfill their own needs. Our emotions drive us.

How to Set Healthy Boundaries

The first step is to be clear about your decision. Can it be changed? If yes, that's fine; you might give in or reach common ground. If not, you need to be prepared.

When you want to stand firm as a rock:

1. Make your decision clear.

2. Look at what you fear. If you have made a decision that you stand by, consider everything you fear while holding onto that decision.

3. Face the fear. What is the worst thing that can happen? Can you live with that and manage? If the answer is yes, you can stand by your decision. If not, you need to find out what the options are. Ask yourself, will it kill me? The brain's deepest fear is dying, and without us knowing it, this is usually the deepest layer of emotion that holds us back from standing up for ourselves.

4. When you have examined your fear, begin to write down the situations where you find it hard to stick to your decisions. Look at the people you interact with and narrow down if there is a person-

ality type you find it hard to say no to. Is it men or women? Is it people who are more skilled than you or older? The more specific you can be, the easier it will be to practice.

5. It's time to practice. In the beginning, set boundaries in harmless situations. Don't start with your boss or someone you have feared for years. Pick an easy situation. It can be that you won't be cooking tonight, that you are not going on a trip, or that you are doing something for yourself. Beginning at home is usually good, and you can also tell your family that you are practicing setting boundaries so they can support you.

6. Keep practicing. Setting boundaries is something that takes time. We can be great at it in one situation but terrible in others. So, practice, observe, and learn from your success. That is the best way to make a strong and solid inner rock you can lean on for the rest of your life.

PART VII

Personality Types
The inner strategy

25

WHAT IS YOUR INNER STRATEGY?

There are four personality types, each with an inner strategy to communicate, cooperate, and deal with changes, conflicts, and challenges. We all have a preference personality type we use by default. According to psychiatrist C.G. Jung, who conducted the first and most extensive research on personality types, we begin observing our surroundings when we are born. The basic needs for a human to survive are to feel safe and get food, drink, and care. We develop strategies to fulfill our basic needs, and when we reach the age of six, we begin to develop the first of our personality types—our *preference*. From observing our closest family, we unconsciously decide which personality will be most suitable to develop. We look at our parents and siblings, and depending on their personality types, we try to create a balance in the family. Then, we begin to practice the strategy. We do it in our behavior, communications, and our decision-making. As we grow up, it becomes a part of us, like an inner compass that sets the direction in everything we do. We practice our preferred personality type solely until we reach age twelve. Then, we know our strategy well and have the surplus to develop our supporting strategy —the one that will help our preference and, if needed, take over. We practice this strategy until the beginning of our twenties. Then, most people are ready to widen their horizons again and begin to stretch to learn new strategies. From the early twenties until our mid-thirties, we practice a third one. And from our mid-thirties until we get close to fifty, we practice the fourth and last.

I meet many people who tell me that they feel more grounded when they reach their fifties. The reason is that they usually know all four strategies and can easily use them in the most appropriate ways. No matter which personality type you prefer, everybody can draw upon all four personality qualities, and in principle, we can develop all four equally. I have never met anyone who has done so, but it is possible. When working with personality types, it's always good to begin by determining your balance in the four personality types. Then, you will know your inner strategy and drive and what is more challenging for you. The next step is to discover how well the four strategies are developed inside you. The more access you have to the four strategies, the easier it is to understand people with different preferences than you but also use the strategies where they are most suitable.

Many children have primitive conflicts in preschool. One personality type will push away another kid if under pressure. Another will withdraw and analyze the situation. The third type will become insecure, and the fourth will think outside the box and come up with solutions. These are the four different strategies we use from an early age. The problem in our younger years is that we only have one strategy we can use, and we don't understand the others. When we begin to develop the second one, the character of the conflicts tends to change. Now, we have two strings to play. Not all people develop more than two strategies; if they are not challenged and find that using only one or two works for them, why bother? That can make it hard for them to understand other people and see the perspective others have on a matter when they grow up. When you get older and might get an education or a job, you have to deal with new situations and different people. It's a good time to develop a greater understanding of perspectives that are different than your own, and it's needed if you want to avoid conflicts and manage to cooperate. But not all people care about personal development, and if you stop learning about yourself and making progress in your personality, you will find it hard to stretch and understand where other people are coming from and respect that we are different. Most people experience many changes from their early twenties to mid-thirties, so learning about the third type is convenient. You graduate, get a job, meet someone, fall in love, and start a family. From your mid-thirties until you reach fifty, you have a long stretch again when you learn and practice your personality types. You test them in different situations, and you realize that it can be beneficial to understand others' personality types to get along and create great results or help a family function.

We usually talk and act according to our personality type if we are unaware of it. It's easy, and it's what we have learned. When we become aware of our personality type, we can look at the other person and address our communications to their personality type. In that way, the other person will feel more seen and understood. If we are unaware of our personality type, we will use our preferences to communicate and can easily feel misunderstood or struggle to get the message through to the other person. There are several different ways to categorize people into personality types. Psychiatrist C.G. Jung's work has laid the foundation for personality tests like the JTI and Insights. Another personality analysis is the DISC based on William Moulton Marston's theories from 1928, which he presented for the first time in his book *Emotions of Normal People*. After working with people and personal development for many years, I realized there is a link between Jung's research and the ancient wisdom of the East, like reflexology, acupuncture, and feng shui. Based on all the pearls of wisdom and the insights into how the brain has developed, I created a brain-smart way to work with personality types that is true to Jung's research and aligned with Eastern wisdom. I call it the Essence personality type. The Essence tool is created so it's easy to use and remember, and on top of that, when you become familiar with the types, you will be able to see which types your children are, your spouse, friends, and colleagues. When I visit companies and ask if they work with personality types, most say yes and then confirm they have forgotten all about it. With the Essence tool, you will understand other people's reactions, see through conflicts in your life, and become much wiser.

Personality types don't tell us anything about whether you are a kind person, if you lie, or if you will succeed or not. But it tells you a lot about your approach to a new task, how you deal with change, react under pressure, and communicate.

The Essence tool provides an exact and tangible insight into an individual's personality type and the personality type's opportunities and challenges. The personality type model can be used at many levels and is not limited to just the personality type. When working in depth with the Essence tool, you will gain a deep understanding of your full potential and what can block you from fully realizing your talent.

Knowledge of personality types can be used to create optimal communication, assemble the best teams, optimize company changes, and minimize misunderstandings. You will also be able to understand conflicts in your family, how to approach your children, and why you get along better with one of your children than another.

Based on your personality type, you can look at internal balances and imbalances and use them for personal development.

When we know our personality type, we better understand our way of handling situations, both those we handle easily and those that challenge us. Through working with personality types, we can better understand other personality types and their different ways of viewing and dealing with situations. This can lead to greater inclusiveness and an increased focus on our own and others' strengths and resources.

All the personality types are equally valuable, each with strengths and qualities. However, all the types can experience imbalance if they use their strengths too much. To create balance in a team, a representative from each type needs to be present. But since most people bring their preference and supporting type, two people can make up a great team.

Typically, an individual feels confident using the skills and strategies from two personality types, but everyone has the potential to tap into the qualities of all four types. By default, you primarily utilize the strengths of the two types that define your character. However, in various situations and when interacting with different people, you can also draw on qualities from other types. By recognizing which types resonate most with you and which ones you are challenged by, you can practice accessing the qualities of the remaining types. It requires a conscious effort and will only be successful with practice.

There are some key features you can look for when you are curious about personality types. If you know and remember these, you are off to a great start using the wisdom actively in your life, and you can begin to make significant improvements.

- **The Doer** will always try to get things done fast. They are often efficient and impatient.

- **The Thinker** likes to know all the facts before making a decision. They often need more information and time to think.

- **The Feeler** seeks unity and can be challenged by speed and lack of empathy.

- **The Changer** loves to make changes and strives to make a difference in the world. You will often hear them say, could this also be a possibility?

DOER   THINKER   FEELER   CHANGER

If we turn back time to the human development in the African Savannah, the Doer will say, "I'm hungry; let's get some food." And then they will take off. On the savannah, they might stop and look at each other and say, "Where are the animals?" Everybody shrugs. Then the fastest one says, "Don't worry, let's run this way," so they run only to find another empty field. Finally, they manage to find some animals and then look at each other. "Did you bring any weapons?" one asks the other, who shakes his head. "Then what do we do?" "Well, let's just knock them out." Luckily, the Thinker was developed, and their approach is slightly different. They will grab hold of the Doers before they take off and say, "Hey, let's do some research before you take off." "Research," the Doer would reply, "that is slow and boring!" But soon they realized that it was clever too. The Thinker worked out where the animals were at different times of day, their body fat percentage, which track belonged to which animal, and what weapons to bring. Now, they could send the Doer off hunting. But it wasn't perfect yet. Then, the Feelers came forward. "Let's find out who is good at what, so everybody knows what they are doing. Who will watch the fire, do the tracking, and shoot a bow and arrow?" They made sure everybody felt seen and heard and supported each other. Theoretically, these three types could survive together, but we wouldn't be here today without the last type, the Changer. The Changer will always try to improve things and focus on the greater good for everybody. So, they invented a system where they could shoot not just one animal a day but two or three and then store the meat during the winter when there were fewer animals to find. In that way, the human species developed, and through the years, the balance between the types has been essential for any process to succeed.

Let's examine the different types, and as you read on, try to observe which type you can relate to the most. You will find personality features from all four, but which one is more you? Remember not to look for what you would like to be, but be honest and go with your first instinct. If you want to test yourself later, you can download our free Essence Personality test app.

App Store

Google Play

26

DOER—FAST AND DECISIVE

DOER

Doers are the active, fast, and often outgoing types. They make things happen, preferring to act first and analyze later. They often juggle multiple tasks and love to set things in motion. A great day for a Doer is when they get a lot off their hands. They love moving forward and hate to stand still. They quickly get bored and impatient.

Personality Traits

- Seeks influence
- Willing to take responsibility
- Motivated by competition
- Likes to make decisions and be decisive
- High status is often important
- May pursue personal gain in tasks
- Individualistic

Doers typically have magnetic personalities, capturing attention when they enter a room because of their inner "fire." Many doers are passionate about what they do and always willing to put in the extra effort required to achieve their goals. They have an innate drive and high energy levels. Sometimes, they can appear dominating to others, who might feel they are "too much." Doers rarely see themselves this way; instead, they might wonder why others cannot keep up with their pace.

A Doer always likes to have a say in a matter, and to avoid conflicts, hear them out and make them feel like they decided something. It doesn't matter if it's big or small; they need a win. If you live or work with a Doer, make sure if you make a decision, that you give them a say in the matter; otherwise, they will try to prevent it or become negative. You can set the framework and give them small things to decide on—things that are unimportant to you. Let's say you make the meal plan, but the family can choose which day they want each meal. At work, you decided that the team should all be at the office one day a week. Which day is up to them to decide. In that way, you involve others and make them participate in the change or task, and Doers love taking responsibility. It is one of their motivational drivers.

When they go shopping, they love to bargain or get something for free; when they succeed, they are so happy. Young Doers especially like to keep an argument going until they win; older ones usually soften up a bit.

Doers have another great motivational driver: competition. They love winning, which releases dopamine in their brain, a hormone that makes us happy. Doers hate when people say *it's not about winning but participating*. They couldn't disagree more. It's all about being the best at what you do and winning. When they go grocery shopping, they compete with the people in the other line to reach the checkout first, and on the highway, in a queue, they compete with the cars in the other lane. Some Doers are unaware of this inner drive to win, but if you believe you are a Doer, look for it. It will make you understand yourself a lot better.

If a Doer finds that another person waffles, they cut through and make a decision. They can quickly turn into alpha males (or females) and make decisions they don't have the authority to make, but they can't help themselves. When they talk, they expect you to listen. It is crucial for them to feel that they have a high status and that you respect them. While they love competing, they also love winning, which can be a blind spot for them. They are not that great at team-work or sharing. They prefer to hold the trophy and take the win.

I'm a Doer, and even though I know, it is still my way of acting and thinking. I'm the only Doer in my family, and since we all know it, we can make fun of it. I make fast decisions and don't think about stuff for long. The other day, I asked my son if it would be a good idea for him to get his own electric toothbrush for the bathroom downstairs next to his room. He nodded. A few days later, he said to me, "Mom, I thought about it, and I would like the toothbrush you mentioned when it's possible." I looked at him and said, "I ordered it two days ago."

In my world, why wait? Let's get it done and move on; there's no need to think too much. I have learned to be patient because I'm the only Doer in my family. When we bought our house six years ago, we saw it, and I just knew I wanted it. If it were up to me, we would have signed the papers immediately to ensure no one else bought it before us. I know my partner is a Thinker, and they need to think a bit more, so I didn't say anything all day. When we had dinner, I thought it was about time to discuss it; I had been so patient all day, giving her space to think. "So, what do you think? Should we buy it?" I asked. She looked surprised and thought it was an unserious question... impossible to answer.

In Headlines:

- Goal-oriented
- Individual achievement
- Seek Freedom
- Enjoy challenges
- Confident
- Competitive
- Demanding
- Direct communication

If you are a Doer, you will recognize the drive to strive for more (success). You love chasing a goal and winning. Being the best at what you do makes you happy, but you also seek freedom. You don't want anyone telling you what to do or how to do it. You will figure it out. In that sense, you are more comfortable working independently and taking responsibility than the other profiles. You will get things done and move forward. When working with others, you demand that they also take responsibility, and if they don't, it can irritate you tremendously, and you will most likely do it yourself and not count on them again. At home, this can mean that you do the cleaning, laundry, or cut the lawn—when it's needed, you do it, and you can't wait around for the others to get started. You end up with a lot of tasks because you're fast and also, to a certain extent, enjoy getting things done your way. And when you do it yourself, you're sure to get it done in time and properly.

Out of Balance

When a Doer overuses their natural abilities, they become dominating and can become overly aggressive. They can easily steamroll others and lose touch with other people's feelings and the situation.

An off-balance Doer can get "tunnel vision" and lose perspective. They can only see their solution and have difficulty listening to others. When out of balance, they can become impatient and lose their grounding; they make decisions that are not thought through to survive and leave others behind in their eagerness to succeed.

If Doers cannot find passion in their work or hobby, their inner fire diminishes. The same happens if they are forced to be slow and always hold back to give others space.

When I was a young Doer, people often told me I was too fast. They couldn't keep up, and I wasn't always popular. When I played handball, I was the best on the team, and everybody knew that if it weren't for me, we wouldn't win. They could always play me, and I would score a goal. But I wasn't great at including others in the game or making great assists. I wanted to belong more and began practicing being slow. I waited for others, stopped taking too much responsibility, and slowly lost myself and my inner drive. The fire inside of me was extinguished. I didn't care about anything and just went along until one day, I realized it wasn't either or. I could find a balance in the middle; sometimes, I could be fast, and I learned to be patient. Now, I have discovered a way to use my strength in a balanced way.

Learning Points

- Meditation (inner peace and reflection)
- Research before acting
- Learn to work together as a team/family

If we want to get the most out of our personality type, it is essential to balance it. If you find that you sometimes overuse it or use the unbalanced sides of it, you can learn to find balance in focusing on three things.

Meditation is, for many Doers, the most boring thing to do. It feels like a millstone around your neck. But to balance being fast without shutting down, the ability to meditate and take deep breaths is important. When you learn, you will see that your Doer will be even more useful since you use the strength and not imbalance. Many Doers forget to research and be patient, which can lead to saying or doing things they regret, or they find that the results are not as good as possible. Taking the time to look into the matter will balance it. Since Doers are driven by winning and succeeding, it is important that they realize that a team can help them. Nobody can win the great bike race, The Tour De France, alone. They need people who support them when riding in a crosswind and over the mountains, and they need people to guide them, cook, and look after the bikes and riders that are by their side. We are all dependent on someone else, and we can all learn from others. When the Doer comes to terms with that, they will see that their win is not less valuable because others supported them. Now, they also have someone to celebrate the victory with. The sooner a Doer learns to let go sometimes and let others offer their help, the sooner they will feel more balanced.

As a strong Doer, I have learned to balance my urge to act quickly with the need to give others space. I also know that the Feeler type (who tends to move more slowly) can provoke me, especially when they are out of balance. Understanding this helps me manage my emotions when I start to feel upset and impatient; instead of reacting, I can smile and practice patience.

Famous Doers:

Steve Jobs: Known for his intensity, demanding nature, and focus on results.

Michael Jordan: He is considered one of the greatest basketball players of all time, and was known for his competitiveness, decisiveness, and ability to lead his team to victory. His relentless drive on and off the court, as well as his impatience for anything less than excellence, exemplifies the "Doer" personality.

Greta Thunberg: She has become a prominent climate activist. Her direct, no-nonsense communication style and ability to mobilize and lead a global movement at a young age indicates a strong Doer.

Jeff Bezos: The founder of Amazon, is known for his decisive and strategic approach to business. His focus on rapid growth and innovation, along with his ability to execute complex plans quickly, aligns with the "Doer" mindset. His intense drive and sometimes uncompromising nature also reflect the out-of-balance traits of impatience and assertiveness.

27

THINKER—STRUCTURE AND PERSPECTIVE

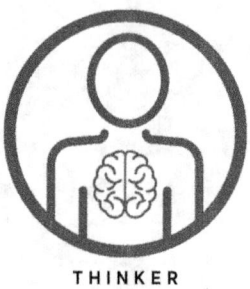

THINKER

Thinkers are people who love to be in control. They like to plan ahead and often have systems and structures they rely on. They are detail-oriented and like to have time to research and know all the facts before making a decision. Many Thinkers like Excel and are specialists in their field of work. They are rarely pioneers and prefer that others try out new things before they do it themselves. Thinkers think logically and find it hard to deal with things that don't add up or can't be put into a formula like emotional intelligence.

Personality Traits

- Need for immersion
- Values evidence, references, and research
- Often good at overview and structure
- Prefers to separate work and personal life
- Favors thorough planning
- Investigates matters deeply before making decisions
- Conscientious and reliable

Thinkers like to have time to get the complete picture of a task before they begin, and then they prefer to have time to dive into the subject and look at all perspectives. They use their common sense and like evidence-based conclusions. Thinkers are good at analyzing and are often rational thinkers. They can spend a long time getting all the details and are often perfectionists. If they have a hobby, they will likely know all aspects of the matter. And if they are buying something for their hobby, they will do thorough research before deciding what to get. Rushing things or giving others a quick answer without having time for preparation can stress them. They value research and evidence and rely on facts, not a gut feeling. They find that frivolous. If you invite them to a meeting but forget to include an agenda, they don't know what to prepare for and find it unprofessional. Never ask them to jump in and take over a presentation if they haven't had time to prepare. They usually won't say anything unless they are 100 percent sure; therefore, they can carry a lot of knowledge they don't share. You might find that they don't say anything at meetings or dinners and see them as dull and introverted, but this might not be true. They might be thinking about a matter and are not ready to say anything; they wait until they are sure. A Thinker can seem quiet and closed off because, often, they are thinking about a matter and making plans inside their head. They prefer to work at work and are not keen on hearing about your pet or sick child; they are there to deliver on a high level. You can count on them when you ask them to investigate a case. They will look at all possible angles and solutions, and if you ask about something, make sure to have time to listen to their findings. When working with a Thinker, setting a deadline is good; otherwise, they will keep looking deeper into the matter and never finish. They strive for perfection.

Thinkers prefer well-documented matters, and all facts must be in place. When you share knowledge with them, expect them to inquire about your sources and the basis for your presentation and opinions. Some Thinkers can become "nerdy" with their knowledge, in a good way, because they take pride in being the best in their field and delve deeply into the subject matter. But that can also prevent them from living their dream. Let's say you are a Thinker and want to be self-employed and offer your service to others. You are great at online marketing, but before you can allow yourself to teach and help others, you need to be sure you know everything and that no one can hold a candle to your work. Needing to be perfect and the unconscious fear of not being good enough or other people's opinions can hold you back.

My youngest son is a Thinker. A couple of years ago, my dad asked him if he wanted a basketball net for the garden. He said he wasn't sure. A year later, he told me he had thought about it and would love to have one. Should he tell his grandad? "Yes," I said, "but maybe mention that you have thought about it for a year and ask if the offer still stands."

In Headlines:

- Rational
- Systematic
- Detail oriented
- Clarity
- Overview
- Demanding
- Specialist

If you are a Thinker, you are likely to have a practical approach to any assignment—whether at home or work. You are organized and like to make structures. When you go shopping, you have a long list; when you need to do something, you like to be prepared and organized. When my son had saved up for a new computer, he researched all the different parts for months. Every day, he checked if the price had changed or if there was an update to any product. He watched YouTube videos and read documentation to ensure the parts he bought would be the perfect combination. And when he was able to get everything he wanted, he bought it and spent a day building the computer. Within six months, he became a specialist in building computers, and even his big brother (who is nine years older) was amazed. The satisfaction was tremendous the moment he turned it on, and everything worked as planned. He was twelve years old at the time. He used all the abilities above to build the perfect computer.

As mentioned earlier, I'm a Doer and live with a Thinker. When we were looking for a house, and I was ready to buy it right away, I knew that my partner was a Thinker, and I had to show consideration; otherwise, I would never get her on board. My inner strategy was pushing me to ask what she thought about the house and if she thought we should buy it. Her inner strategy needed all the details, pros, and cons; she needed to talk to the bank, and she needed time. We often joke about it because it is so obvious that we have different strategies to act and make decisions. We made an offer a few days later and closed the deal within three weeks, which was our luck since more buyers turned up. If it weren't for my ability to act fast, we wouldn't have gotten the house, but with her ability to put the brakes on now and again, we were also sure it was the right decision, and all the details were in place.

Out of Balance

- Controlling
- Arrogant
- Look down on others

When Thinkers overuse their talent, they can come across as cold and arrogant. They might look down on others who do not seem as "smart" as themselves and can even undermine colleagues or family if they are unprepared. My dad is a Thinker, and I remember when I was a child, we played cards in the evening on weekends. One night, my dad asked me, "Why are you playing that card when the other aces have already been played?" I looked at him, puzzled. "How do you know?" He looked at me arrogantly, "Because I'm counting the cards." I had never thought about that possibility; I was just playing the game. I felt so stupid and somehow also betrayed. Here I was naïve and thought we were just having a family game, but he was analyzing and determined to win. (He is both a Doer and a Thinker).

Thinkers can appear harsh and dismissive. They do their part of the job and expect others to do the same. Thinkers would rather work alone than collaborate with those they perceive as less competent.

When they don't feel that others are meeting their expectations, they can talk down to them or make them feel useless. Some of the other personality types can become afraid of the Thinkers when they are out of balance and withdraw. It can stress them, and instead of asking questions or focusing on what they are good at, they pull away from the person. The unbalanced Thinker can be merciless and pedantic.

Many Thinkers struggle to deal with their own and others' emotions. Emotions are intangible, making them hard to grapple with. Thinkers may have shut off their feelings unconsciously, causing them to be easily challenged in times of change. They seek logical explanations for their reactions, aiming to keep control of the situation, which can make them seem cold and arrogant during transitional phases, especially when others might be showing their emotions and vulnerabilities.

Thinkers are not insensitive; they have learned to guard their emotions and find that emotions are unnecessary when delivering their message. They might even blur it. So, they have learned that it is appropriate to suppress them. This occurred at an early stage in their lives when they experienced that their feelings had not been acknowledged or accepted. In such situations, they might have been praised for their knowledge and ability to handle the situation.

Behind the perhaps hard and intelligent façade, you might find someone who also needs contact with others and needs to be recognized for qualities other than those that belong to the Thinker. This is something that Thinkers may discover when they become older. I have met many Thinkers who are hard and decisive. Sometimes, they are even brutal in their relationships with others. They focus on numbers and statistics. Personal growth and caring about whether people thrive doesn't interest them. They will categorize meditation and spirituality as bogus and a waste of time. However, one day, they might find that their strategy is insufficient. It doesn't work anymore, especially if they are challenged in life. Then, they are forced to open up to other parts of themselves and begin to use other strategies.

I know many leaders who tell me they missed their kid's upbringing or didn't have a close relationship with them because their Thinker strategy was out of balance. I had a leader attending one of my lectures, and the first thing he said when presenting himself was: "I don't like people." I was astonished and thought: You are a leader. In my opinion, the most significant responsibility of a leader is to lead people. During the day, we worked with different tools and insights, and by the end of the day, he said: "Now I know why I don't like people. I've been afraid of their reactions. What if a colleague begins to cry or tells me something I don't know how to deal with?" He took a deep breath, "I feel so much better now, and you know what? I think I'm beginning to like people."

Being a Thinker in a company going through changes can sometimes be challenging. Thinkers prefer things to be well-documented and researched, which is not always the case with changes. Moreover, Thinkers thrive when given time to immerse themselves in tasks, and turbulent changes can worsen their working conditions. This can push the Thinker into imbalance. This is also the case at home. If a Thinker is forced into a change or difficult situation for which they are not prepared, it can be highly challenging for them. These situations could include becoming ill, losing their job, or getting divorced. If they are about to move, they will do everything in their power to plan ahead, and the things they cannot predict can be quite stressful and overwhelming.

Learning Points

- Trust over control
- Adjust ambitions
- Conclude

If you are a Thinker and want to balance your ability as a Thinker, the most important lesson is to begin to let go of control slowly. It can be practiced in many different situations, like cooking. Try not to follow the recipe to the letter; let go a little. Improvise. When you go to a meeting, don't prepare 120%. Ask yourself, when is it good enough? This also applies when you are cleaning at home and feel the urge to intervene because others are not meeting your standards. It can be difficult for you not to redo their work or say something.

Many Thinkers have such high ambitions that they are never satisfied. It can be hard work—always trying to be perfect. And remember, it's rooted in fear—the fear of not being good enough, the fear of other people's reactions, or the fear of losing control.

As a Thinker, it can be a great help sometimes to ask yourself, is this good enough? Does it have to be perfect for you to feel satisfied? Choose the projects that are important to you and go all in, and then choose the ones where it is okay to do what you are paid for or have the time to do. Many Thinkers work in their free time because then they feel better when handing over a project. But if a customer won't pay for your time, don't. Other people begin to take your time for granted and calculate that you are using your free time to work. It's a slippery slope, and you will eventually lose not only your free time but also your motivation. When I said that to a woman the other day, she replied, but we are paid 1:1 for our extra time. Great, I said, but how will you get back the time you missed out on with your friends, family, and kids 1:1? You can't. And slowly, we lose touch with ourselves and work even more to feel a kind of satisfaction and justify it with excuses.

Finally, it's great to learn to conclude your projects when you are a Thinker. This is it; I'm done. Many Thinkers will go on and on improving, looking for more evidence or refining details. You have to learn when it is good enough. Do some things with perfection and learn to enjoy those that are not. My girlfriend hates the weeds between our tiles in the garden. And we have so many tiles. I agree that it doesn't look good. But it takes forever to clean them out, and we have to start all over again when we're done. We have lived in our house since 2018 and have never managed to keep them nice and clean all summer. I had to tell her to let go and focus on what we can manage. We have made so many great improvements to the house, and we don't have time to keep everything perfect. It is a learning process. If we always strive for perfection, we will miss life itself.

Famous Thinkers:

Stephen Hawking: Theoretical physicist known for his contributions to cosmology and quantum gravity.

Bill Gates: Co-founder of Microsoft and philanthropist known for his strategic thinking and technological innovations.

Ada Lovelace is considered the first computer programmer, known for her analytical approach to mathematics and her foresight in seeing the potential of computing machines. Her ability to understand and articulate complex ideas about technology makes her a notable "Thinker."

Albert Einstein was a theoretical physicist known for his groundbreaking theories on relativity and his profound impact on modern science. His ability to think deeply about abstract concepts and analyze complex ideas makes him a quintessential "Thinker."

28

FEELER—INTUITIVE AND EMPATHETIC

FEELER

Feelers listen to their feelings and often sense the mood and how others are doing. They are in touch with their emotions and emphasize that decisions should feel right. It's important to Feelers that we treat each other well, and they find joy in helping other people. When making a decision, they need time to feel if it's right for them and aligned with their values. They are sensitive to negative people and can work hard to ensure everybody feels good. Feelers thrive in the company of others and enjoy working with friends or colleagues on a project. They can get insecure if they don't know what is happening and will often compare themselves with others.

Personality Traits

- Needs predictability
- Time to reflect
- Caring toward others
- Prefers collaboration over working alone
- Often loyal and helpful
- Needs a positive environment
- Security is important for their well-being

As a Feeler, you enjoy being a part of a group or a family. Belonging is essential for you to feel safe. Feelers care about other people and will go far to ensure everybody feels good and is happy. They can sense how other people are feeling and feel secure when they know they can trust other people. If they go to a concert or out for dinner, they prefer to go with others. Going by themselves will make them feel insecure and uncomfortable. Feelers don't have more feelings than the other personality types, but they relate to their feelings more. The feeling is a reference for them; they won't do it if things don't feel good. That is also why they need to know what is happening... so they feel safe. When they experience change, it's essential that the change feels good and that they feel included to go along with the change. Sometimes, they must also sleep on it before deciding on a matter. That can make them seem a little slow, and especially the Doer needs to be patient with the Feeler; otherwise, the Feeler will feel stressed out and become insecure.

The Feeler quality helps make healthy relationships, and since they are in touch with their emotions, they can show vulnerability and make deep connections with others. Sometimes, Feelers see this as a weakness, but it couldn't be further from the truth. Many people have vulnerability wired as a weakness in their brain, so they think if they show emotions, they are weak. This is a leftover from another generation, and luckily, many young people don't have this wiring in their brains. We can all rewire our brains; when you become aware of a limitation and limiting connections, it is good to rewire it.

Building healthy relations will be one of the superpowers companies will look for in the future. When we feel good at work, have strong ties, and feel supported, we are more likely to stay in our jobs longer, and we will support our colleagues. We talk to others about our workspace in a positive way, and it will be easier for the company to attract new employees. The young generation will not put up with a poor work climate, lousy leadership, or a lack of meaningfulness.

In Headlines:

- Empathetic
- Team players
- Sensitive
- Thorough
- Loyal
- Listening
- Patient

Feelers often have their "hearts in the right place" and act as "social glue" in the workplace or family. They arrange company events, organize Secret Santa, or facilitate a glass of wine in the department on Friday afternoons. They look after their friends and care for others, so much so that they are willing to have less for themselves as long as others feel good. My mother is a Feeler. She is retired and doesn't have much money, but in the wintertime, she would rather save on her food so she can afford to buy food for the birds in the garden. It gives her joy to look after others and be there for others—humans and animals.

Feelers will go to great lengths to avoid conflicts. If a conflict arises, they retreat or try to smooth things out. Feelers prefer a positive work environment; if it is not positive, they will withdraw and, in the end, look for a job elsewhere. Many Feelers are also scared of confronting others if they don't agree or feel hurt; they hope it will pass or go away. But it rarely does. They pile up their emotions inside and begin to blame themselves instead of taking responsibility and letting others know how they feel.

They are great listeners, and other people tend to take advantage of them—especially the ones whining. Many Feelers have difficulty setting boundaries and will listen to the whining day after day. Instead of saying no, they will begin to come to work earlier or work from home to avoid the person.

At work, many Feelers see their team as their second family. They know all about each other and love to talk about their kids or pets. To them, it's natural to show pictures from their holidays, and they feel safe when they know the people they are working with. Feelers make decisions based on their personal values and not on science—it has to feel good. What they offer cannot be measured in the same way as a Thinker's work. But that doesn't make it less valuable. On the contrary, when we thrive and feel good, we tend to produce better results and help each other succeed.

Out of Balance

- Become uncertain
- Sudden changes
- Low self-esteem

When Feelers are not seen and recognized for their skills, their self-confidence can be affected. This may make them overly contact-seeking, as they need to make sure they are good enough or handling tasks correctly. They will ask you about the same thing several times or be overly sensitive about your body language or tone of voice and assign more value to it than you are aware of. They might come across as clingy, but they need affirmation, as their core strength—their emotions—have not been acknowledged in some way or are out of balance. It's easy to become annoyed with them and push them away. This is the worst way to deal with a Feeler out of balance. Instead, listen to them with presence, acknowledge how they feel, and let them know you are okay. If you have an issue, tell them it's your business, and they don't need to worry. Make sure that they understand their part of it and that you take responsibility for yours. Never lie to a Feeler; they build their relationships on trust, and when the trust is broken, or they think it is, they begin to make up stories and become insecure. The insecurity can eat them up and turn into anxiety, thinking they are not capable of dealing with the situation.

A former colleague always talked through her emotions, and the more she did, the more irritated I got. All I could hear was how unfair things were, and when she needed help, she always played the victim. Being a Doer, it was like waving a red cloth in my face. When working with a Doer, you need to take responsibility; otherwise, the Doer will run you over. So, I had to take many deep breaths to keep the inclination under control. Also, she was so slow. Before making a decision, she had to go over the issues so many times and kept asking the same questions. I would have run her over if I didn't know about personality types. But knowing this was just an inner strategy when she felt pressured, I could help her return to her resources and believe in herself. Mind you, it's not always easy to support others since their imbalance can provoke you to be out of balance, too.

The worst thing that can happen to Feelers is having to work with a Thinker who is out of balance. They feel incompetent and outright stupid when paired with a harsh, heartless thinker colleague, boss, or spouse.

Changes can seem overwhelming if Feelers are out of balance. They will doubt themselves and their abilities. They will need significantly more time to accept changes as they can greatly impact them.

If you recognize the traits of a Feeler within yourself, it is crucial that you own them! As a feeler, you might easily downplay your abilities and think others are more competent than you. Recognize your needs in times of change and stand firm about them. Staying true to yourself and being aware of how your emotions affect you is essential. You must find a strong, healthy foundation to excel in what you do best.

Learning Points

- Stand up for oneself
- Set boundaries and speak up
- Put oneself before others

The most important learning point to balance the Feeler strategy is setting boundaries. I can't emphasize this enough. Feelers need to learn to take care of themselves in order to support others. And they also need to be respected. When we always say yes and put ourselves second, others take us for granted. Slowly, the respect for you and what you offer will be gone, and you will begin to feel the same way and talk yourself down. To regain respect, you must set boundaries and sometimes say no. Know how far you are willing to go to help others, and make sure you look after yourself too. Be clear that you would love to help, but you need to finish your own tasks first—or you can help next week, not today.

A leader told me he had a Feeler as a personal assistant. He was so embarrassed when he learned about the personality types. He said, "I give my assistant all the tasks I can't be bothered to do myself, and I don't respect her. I take her for granted, and she is always so good to me. But the better she treats me, the less I respect her. I will tell her to set boundaries and say no to me."

Usually, it is the fear of being excluded that drives the Feeler to say yes. They are afraid of not surviving on their own and will do anything to belong. And that can backfire if others find out. Some people will take advantage of it, and there have been many cases in the past several years with MeToo, especially with rich and powerful men who take advantage of women who had a hard time saying no.

Feelers have to take care of themselves before helping others, and they need to risk becoming unpopular when standing up for themselves. A leader I have known for over five years told me that the most important thing for him as a leader was that everybody liked him. I hated breaking the news to him, but I had to tell him it wasn't possible. But he shouldn't let go of his values and ability to care. He needed to balance it. He found the courage to make decisions that others didn't agree with and stand up for himself, using his ability to care for and make people work together at the same time.

Famous Feelers:

Princess Diana: Former Princess of Wales known for her humanitarian work and empathy toward marginalized communities.

Oprah Winfrey: Media mogul and philanthropist known for her empathetic interviewing style and efforts to promote personal growth and well-being.

John Lennon: A member of The Beatles, was known for his advocacy for peace, love, and understanding. His music and activism were deeply rooted in empathy and a desire to promote harmony and social change, reflecting his "Feeler" personality.

Martin Luther King Jr.: A civil rights leader driven by a profound sense of justice, compassion, and empathy. His commitment to non-violence and his ability to deeply connect with and inspire others reflect his strong "Feeler" nature, as he sought to create a world based on love and equality.

29

CHANGER—FLEXIBLE AND READY FOR CHANGE

CHANGER

Changers thrive when new initiatives arise and are good at adapting. They quickly become bored without progression or momentum in activities. Changers strive to be a force for good; their perspective is rarely selfish, and they are motivated to improve the world. They are easygoing and don't want too many fixed appointments on their calendar; it's nice to be spontaneous. They find it easy to meet new people and are often good fun to be with. They are visionaries and find it easy to think outside the box.

Personality Traits

- Loves changes or development
- Often visionaries and think big
- Likes to make a positive difference for others
- Quick to see the possibilities
- Thinks outside the box
- Often thrives outside their comfort zone
- Needs space for idea development and brainstorming

Changers find it easy to talk to other people and usually have a sense of humor that they use to make others feel good. They are great talkers and like to connect with others. They have a deep inner drive for making progress in everything they do. One important thing to hold onto is that the Changer doesn't do it to gain fame or become rich; they do it because they are driven by meaningfulness and want to make a difference. It can be in a family, where they help provide what is needed for a child; it can be developing a system at work that can help co-workers or the invention of something that will help the world progress with the green transition or illnesses.

They are often curious and look for possibilities when presented with a change. One way to recognize a Changer is by listening to what they say. You often hear them say, "Maybe we could try this out?" they usually question the decisions made and have ideas to improve processes and tasks.

If you ask a Changer to do the same work continuously, they will get bored really fast. They need to feel there is progress in what they do. When you work with a Changer, it is important that you give them some space to think outside the box. If they have a task they need to do, then give them a playground where they can invent new things and let them know how much time they can spend at the playground. Usually, 10-20 percent of their time is enough. If you don't, they will become bored and begin to change things you do not want to be changed, like the code in a computer system, moving the decimal point in the accounts, or pursuing an idea that you told them to let go of. At home, it's the same. They usually love to rearrange the house, have different projects running simultaneously, or find it hard to plan too far ahead. It can be hard for others to keep up or work out what they are up to. A lot of their ideas are in their head, and they are not always great at involving others. They have the ability to look ten years ahead and see what is coming. Just think about it for a moment. If someone told you that one day we would all swipe on our phones before the iPhone was invented, you would have thought that it wasn't possible... or that all cars would be electric one day. There was a whole industry that was caught off-guard.

Changers are often ahead of their time and can find it hard to get others to understand their vision. Even though they exert themselves, getting others to buy in on their ideas can be difficult. Since their mission is to make the world a better place, they also struggle and meet a lot of resistance when it comes to getting their ideas through and financed—because they are first movers and they often run into a Thinker in finance. Luckily, they are like a cork; you can put them underwater, but they will pop right up again, and usually with another take on their vision.

It is important to have different ideas and visions. The Doer is great at finding solutions here and now, and sometimes, it is for their own benefit. Changers always look for opportunities to improve things in the long run—not just a quick fix—but a real change.

When a Changer tries to solve a challenge, they prefer to talk to others. They don't need you to say anything. They talk through the fog and find the solution by speaking out loud. It can be a bit of a strange conversation for you since you just need to listen, and they don't really want your take on the matter. When they find what they are looking for, they will thank you for listening and take off. You might find it a bit strange and not know what you actually helped them with. For the Changer, it is a matter of falling through layers and discovering the solution.

A Changer will often thrive outside their comfort zone. This is where they look into the future. But it can also be challenging, and they can complain a bit. That doesn't mean that you should help them or solve the issue. They need a bit of stress to reach the solutions they are looking for. The best support you can give them is to listen.

Since the Changer is looking to make a positive difference for others, they are often generous people who donate frequently. Their currency is not money but recognition. When they are giving and giving and sometimes out in deep water to find solutions or make things happen, the best way to support them is by seeing their work or vision and praising them for what they do. Recognition will keep them going and is a huge motivational factor for a Changer.

I'm a Changer; it is actually my preference, and my second type is the Doer. When I give lectures or talks, what makes me most happy is the positive feedback from others. My deepest drive is to make a positive difference for others. It's the same with this book; the greatest satisfaction for me is if it can help you improve your life. And the best way to give something back to me, if you feel like it, is to tell others about the book so more people can benefit from the wisdom. If someone posts a picture of the book or writes a review, it makes my day. It is truly the greatest gift. I don't care about making money, which is also a challenge for many Changers; we are willing to give it all away, and we do. I gave away 15,000 copies of my first novel. Some people would say that is crazy, but I long to help others and make a positive difference. I'm grateful if people feel like giving something back, but I don't expect it. I have learned to be better at charging for my services, but I will still do talks and lectures for free if I can see that it will benefit others and my vision. It has been a lifelong learning process to balance my Changer and Doer. I looked up how many places I have lived in my life (we have a national register here in Denmark where you can get information about all sorts of things, including where you have lived.) I have lived in 24 different places in Denmark in my adult life; I have also lived in Australia three times, and I have lived in London (UK). Where we live now is where I have lived the longest as an adult. We bought it in 2018, and it finally feels great to stay in the same place for a longer time. But I can't help myself constantly inventing projects, things we can improve. The great thing about becoming aware of your personality type is that you understand your drive and don't always have to follow it. It is possible to observe it and ask yourself what the best thing to do right now is. I have worked intensely with my personal growth to develop my Feeler and Thinker to create an inner balance. I needed to; otherwise, I would become reckless and never settle down. The personality types are pulling the strings inside of us. Only when you begin to recognize them can you start to develop the other personality strategies and, in that way, balance your life.

In Headlines:

- Flexible
- Constructive
- Humorous
- Spontaneous
- Ready for change
- Optimistic
- Articulate and talkative

If you are a Changer, you will recognize the urge to make changes and create. Many Changers have "popcorn brains." They pop solutions and ideas all the time. However, they also have a hard time working on the same project ffor an extended period unless they see progress and new possibilities.

If someone comes up with an idea, you are quick to buy into it and jump on the train. If it feels right and you can see the vision, there is no need to be critical or ask too many questions. Therefore, many Changers also struggle to make money. They go all in with their savings and take out a loan on their house to make their dream come true. Some succeed, but many don't. Luckily, they don't get depressed that easily and will quickly look for other opportunities.

They enjoy working with others and are often fun to be with. They can easily entertain or tell tales from their life that amaze others (especially Thinkers and Feelers who are a little more withdrawn in their adventurous approach to life). If their favorite football team makes it to the finals, but it is played in another state or country, they might decide that they want to go the evening before. It could also be a concert they hear about at the last minute, and they have an impulse to go. They don't think too much about it; they focus on getting there. Maybe they don't even have tickets. It doesn't matter; they will figure it out when they get there and find a way. They always do. It might not be ideal or what they set out to do, but they will get there. Let's say they are married to a Thinker; the Thinker will begin to ask: Do you have tickets? How will you get there? Where will you stay? How much will it cost? Are you sure you will make it in time?

Can you see the different strategies? It all comes down to our personality type.

For many Changers, their work is not just work; it's their passion. Many Changers are self-employed or in positions where they can develop and have tremendous freedom in their work. They prefer a great deal of flexibility in their lives and are often driven by impulses.

These are people who like to explore new paths, even long before others see the possibility of a path there. Changers usually have abundant energy to innovate; they are valuable assets if changes occur. They willingly shoulder the burden and go the extra mile if they see a purpose behind it.

Out of Balance

- Do as they please
- Encounter resistance to change
- Unrealistic

When a Changer overuses their ability to change or urge to make changes, they can become unrealistic. They lose track of budgets and time. Since they are very passionate about their vision, they can become absorbed by their project and lose sleep, forget to eat, or turn night into day. They don't mind sleeping on the floor or eating leftovers if it means they can continue. That is both a plus and a minus, and sometimes it is what makes them succeed—and sometimes, it leaves them with a great debt for the rest of their lives. They can find it hard to let go or accept that the time is not right or that they have run out of money. They will fight, and it's a great lesson in listening and not getting caught in the vision.

An unbalanced Changer will become disheartened. Instead of a vibrant racehorse, you'll have to deal with a stubborn mule! They will not sabotage changes but will not contribute either. They might develop outright resistance to changes and lower the overall standard only because they have not been heard when suggesting changes or don't see the vision behind the changes.

Changers might adopt an anarchic approach and go their own way, disregarding agreements with others. So, if you agree to do one thing, they might go ahead with their own idea and hope for forgiveness when they might prove you wrong.

A leader in a tech company was a full-blown Changer, and his PA called me for help. She said he fell asleep within five minutes whenever she had a meeting with him. It was impossible for her to run all the things she needed to by him before he was gone. She said they had tried to stand up and even go for a walk, but nothing helped. He couldn't keep focus. I had talked to him a few times since we had also done some teamwork with the company, and he had a high energy level and low focus time. I suggested that she begin to take him for a run instead. That worked. He loved running and getting fresh air, and she got all her questions answered.

Learning Points

- Be realistic
- Get others on board
- Don't identify with the vision

Changers can get engrossed by their vision; to balance that, it is also important to be realistic. It's a balance since being too realistic can kill any new idea. Therefore, it's good for Changers to have friends or family who dare to be honest with them. Let them know if they go too far or their idea is not as great as they believe. It's always hard to see when you get blinded, and Changers can be so excited by their vision that they forget that they have to get others on board, too. It can feel like a punishment if things move too slowly or do not happen as fast as they believe is needed and possible.

When we hear stories about Changers who have made a difference in the world, there is nearly always a story of how they were about to give up, how they were broke, or that no one believed in them. J.K. Rowling sent her manuscript to around 12 publishers before she got accepted. Elon Musk invested a large portion of his personal fortune into Tesla and SpaceX, risking financial ruin if these companies failed. Despite facing setbacks and economic challenges, Musk's determination, innovative vision, and ability to secure investments eventually led to the success of Tesla and his other ventures. Before creating one of the most iconic entertainment companies in the world, Walt Disney faced several rejections and failures. He was once fired from a newspaper for lacking creativity and was told he lacked imagination. He faced bankruptcy and several business failures before finally finding success with the creation of Mickey Mouse and Disneyland. Oprah Winfrey overcame a challenging childhood marked by poverty, abuse, and hardship. She faced numerous obstacles on her path to success, including being fired from her first television job as a news anchor. Despite these setbacks, she persevered and became one of the world's most influential media moguls.

I have learned to be patient and also follow the flow. My vision is to create a higher awareness in the world, and I do it through my books and lectures. When I wrote my first novel, *The Life*, I knew I had to share it with the world. My vision has always been to become a number one *New York Times* bestseller and have my books made into a Netflix series. In the beginning, I risked everything to make it happen. Looking back, I can see I was way ahead of my time. The world wasn't ready. By getting to know my personality strategies, I have been able to balance my life and still hold onto my vision. I believe deep down that I will get there one day, and I take all the steps I can toward it. But I don't know if I will succeed. I know I take responsibility and put my energy and heart into it. I look for every opening but realize that I can't do it alone. I need other people to help and support me. I need others to see what I see. And that is important if you are a Changer; make sure you're not carrying your vision alone. Share it. Trust. And keep taking responsibility. No one knows the timing of the universe, and I know for sure there is no reason to push and fight. Let go and go with the flow. Plant a seed. Water it, give it light. Let it grow at its own pace. Don't pull it, or it will become a skinny tree that will fall over in a storm. Let it grow roots and become strong. When it's ready, other people will stop and enjoy it.

Famous Changers:

Elon Musk: Known for his transformative impact on multiple industries, including electric vehicles, space exploration, and renewable energy. His ambitious projects and entrepreneurial spirit have led to significant advancements and transformations in these fields.

Richard Branson: Known for his bold and adventurous approach to business, Branson has repeatedly disrupted industries and challenged the status quo. His willingness to take risks, innovate, and pivot has led to the success of numerous ventures spanning sectors such as music, aviation, telecommunications, and space travel.

Nelson Mandela: Ahead of his time in his vision for a free and democratic South Africa. His willingness to challenge the status quo and his drive to create a more just and equitable society make him a strong example of the "Changer" type.

Malala Yousafzai: A powerful example of a "Changer" who has taken bold actions to advocate for girls' education and rights around the world. Her courage and drive to make the world a better place, often in the face of danger, highlight her adventurous and change-driven nature.

30

GETTING TO KNOW YOUR PERSONALITY TYPE

Knowing about the four personality types and their strategy can help you get to know yourself and understand your approach and reaction in different situations. When you begin to recognize the inner drive of your personality, you can also start to practice the ones you are not that familiar with to create a balance inside of you. While I'm a Changer and a Doer, I needed to develop the Feeler and Thinker in order to teach all four types. Otherwise, I wouldn't be able to understand or explain my tools to those types. But it was also important for me to achieve an inner balance to create an antipole to the strong Changer and Doer I had developed. If I didn't, I would get into conflicts, find it hard to deal with others, and keep running whenever I meet a challenge.

When you begin looking at yourself, it can be interesting to see how your personality type has influenced your choices and life. Make sure not to blame yourself for your choices; use it to understand yourself and others.

After you recognize your preference (priority type) and your supporter (the second choice), it is time to practice the two less familiar types. Take a look at the outline at the end of the chapter and mark the qualities you possess. Then mark the ones you would like to have. Those are the goals you're working toward now.

Let's say you are a Doer like me and would like more empathy. Then you ask yourself, how can I show more empathy toward my family, friends, or colleagues? Be specific.

- I can tell them I care about them
- I can give them a hug
- I can ask how they are feeling

These are just examples. Make up your own steps and learning points. They must be easy to practice and specific so you know exactly what to do. If you write, I will care more about others. It is too fluffy. Who and how?

If you know a strong Feeler, you can also begin to spend time with this person. That person's strong Feeler will rub off on you, eventually. Being close to that person lets you observe and learn from them, even though they might provoke you initially if you don't have contact with your own Feeler.

Always remember that we tend to use our preferences in times of change, difficult times, and challenging situations. That is actually a time when you would benefit from a balance of the four types so you can use the best strategy and not just the one that comes easiest.

Doer		Thinker
	Goal orientated Success or promotion Individual performance Personal autonomy Decisive Powerful Full of ideas	Rational Systematic Detail oriented Clarity Overview Demanding Specialist	
Impatient **Over powering** **Dominating**		**Controlling** **Arrogant** **Superior**

Changer		Feeler
	Flexible Constructive Sense of humor Spontaneous Ready for changes Optimistic Well formulated and Talkative	Empathic Team player Sensitive Loyal Listeners Patient Thorough	
Do what they want **Can resist changes** **Unrealistic**		**Insecure** **Lose themselves** **Low self esteem**

31

OVERVIEW OF THE PERSONALITY TYPES' RESPONSE TO CHANGE.

(ADVANCED WORK)

Each of the four types has unique reactions to changes, and their reactions differ depending on whether they are in or out of balance.

Doer: Doers are open to change and eagerly welcome new projects and initiatives, especially if they can influence and see a purpose in them.

Doers get upset when they feel initiatives are imposed on them without their input.

Doers may feel the changes are a waste of time if they can't see any meaning or purpose in them. Therefore, communication focusing on "what's in it for me" is important for Doers. If Doers can see a purpose in the change, then you will have strong support for the process.

Thinker: When Thinkers are presented with change, it is a good idea to have a rational and well-thought-out basis for the change. They will probe into the reasoning behind the decision and demand evidence. If you can provide that, they are more likely to accept and support the change.

Thinkers, like Feelers, require a bit more time to adjust. They will not instantly embrace the change as enthusiastically as Doers and Changers might. Therefore, it's important to give Thinkers time to reflect and study the new initiatives and allow them to ask the necessary questions.

If Thinkers perceive changes as a superficial window dressing without a genuinely well-reasoned justification, they will try to prevent them. They can become very harsh and relentless in their rhetoric and opposition.

Feeler: Changes can be challenging depending on how they are presented. Feelers need time to process their feelings and get on board.

If Feelers feel that the new initiatives are being rushed and do not have time to adjust, this can result in stress, confusion, or resignation.

Balanced Feelers are important during change as they will do their best to maintain a good atmosphere and create team or family cohesion.

Feelers are adept at articulating what the change means and how it affects people. They are also good at listening and understanding others' emotional reactions to changes. This way, a more employee-friendly approach to changes can be established. The key requirement for a feeler to embrace change is feeling safe

Changer: Changers love change. They are like racehorses that hate being locked up in a stall.

It's crucial for Changers that there is progress. But even though they thrive in transition, it doesn't necessarily mean they always find it easy. That's why they might complain—especially if things don't turn out as they had envisioned.

Changers prefer to feel influential and not be too restricted. Flexibility and room for innovation are essential for Changers' participation and engagement in the changes. It's important to involve them early in the process; otherwise, they will try to make changes when it's too late.

How the Four Types Live and Work Together

Doer—Doer: Two Doers can usually communicate easily, but they may find themselves competing and both wanting to take the lead. Doers can quickly become unbalanced, and loud conflicts can arise when they trigger each other's imbalance. This personality type finds it the hardest to collaborate with someone of the same type.

When two Doers live or work together, they need to be aware of the risk of being too fast and never researching before making a decision. Neither of them will say, hey, let's sleep on it. They will both say, let's do it right now.

Doer—Thinker: The Doer might struggle with the Thinker's penchant for detail but often has respect for it. Conversely, the Thinker may feel the Doer is too hasty and superficial. However, they can get along, especially when the premise and roles are well-defined, and they aim for the highest standard. They can agree on focusing on the task. In a relationship, you will have the one that makes things happen and the one that makes sure it's the best solution.

Doer —Feeler: The Doer might perceive the Feeler as slow and too "emotional." If things drag on, the Doer can become impatient with too much talk and not enough action. The Feeler will easily feel steamrolled by a Doer. It is essential that they both stretch to understand each other's needs and approach. The Doer and the Feeler are each other's opposites, which is why they can be challenged by each other. When they realize they need each other to balance, they can be the best friends and partners.

Doer—Changer: These two types can easily agree on great ideas and simultaneously motivate each other. They collaborate well, but ensuring they do not just go off on their own tangent, forgetting the team and shared objectives is essential. To have a well-balanced relationship, they need to open up to the Feeler and Thinker side or find someone with these qualities to team up with.

Thinker—Thinker: Two balanced Thinkers can efficiently work together and excel in teams with specialists. They aim to perform at a high level and collaborate with others who share the same mindset and are professionally competent. If two Thinkers are in a relationship, they will most likely take forever to make a decision. They want to move house, but ten years later, they are still unsure where or when. They need to be aware of the risk that pursuing perfection can prevent them from doing anything. They are usually also afraid of regretting... what if it wasn't the right decision? Then it's better to wait.

Thinker—Feeler: Thinkers and feelers can be good for each other if they respect each other. They can agree on time; one needs to think while the other needs to feel. Feelers might struggle in "Thinker teams," while Thinkers would dislike being in "Feeler teams." However, it is important not to underestimate that they need each other to create balance. It is best if an understanding of their different perspectives can be created. In a family, one will be more practical and the other more caring.

Thinker—Changer: The Thinker may struggle to keep up with the Changer's abstract thought processes. Changers are not concerned with sources or facts; they explore and experiment. These two types can greatly benefit from each other, but clear boundaries and objectives must be set for their collaboration to succeed. Both will aim to achieve a high standard. When they live together, they can have a lot of encounters if they are not aware of their inner strategies. The Changer will go with the flow and make changes all the time. The Thinker will try to maintain a structure and schedule. Then the Changer will feel strangled and say it's okay and then do as they wish. That will force the Thinker to control even more. This continues until they become aware of their types and unconscious strategies.

Feeler—Feeler: Feelers love being with other Feelers. They thrive in each other's company. They understand one another and value the same things. The challenge might be that their work environment becomes too much of a "cozy club," and not much gets done, as all the team members are involved in all decisions. When too many Feelers are together, there can also be a lot of gossip and out of balance that can turn into bitching. Feelers need to be aware of not jumping to conclusions based on feelings or making up stories that don't relate to reality. Too many Feelers can make too many assumptions, and combined with feelings, it can become a poison cocktail.

Feeler—Changer: When a Feeler and Changer are together, they can agree that relationships are the most important thing. They both love being with others and are good at sharing.

A Feeler and a Changer will not have significant conflicts or clashes since their competencies do not overlap. They are both interested in others and like to help and support them.

Changer—Changer: Asking multiple Changers to collaborate can be a challenge. They will race ahead at 100 mph—if that is the objective, then all is well. But they won't make a single note and might even forget all their great ideas. If two Changers live together, it can be chaotic. They will most likely face money issues, forget to pay bills, or have many unfinished projects happening simultaneously.

Many people find a person with qualities opposite to themselves in a relationship. In that way, we can also forget to develop the qualities we are missing since we lean on the other. If we get divorced, we will suddenly feel that something is lacking, and it can be harder to cope.

Many people find someone who helps them to balance and then begin to change the person into the personality they are. And then, after ten years, you are too alike, and you get bored and divorced. Remember to respect the other person's personality type and develop your own balance.

Communication with the Other Types

We all prefer to communicate from our preferred type, but you can gain greater understanding if you figure out the personality type you are talking to and address that type in your communication. That way, the other person feels seen, and it's easier for them to understand you. Here are some things you can practice and be aware of when you know which personality type you are dealing with.

When you Communicate with a Doer:

Be clear in your message and touch on a few essential points. Speak clearly and look at the person—show you know what you want. Remember to let them know "what is in it for them." Why should they do it? If you get them engaged, they will be a great support for you.

Avoid:
   - Getting into too many details.
   - Too many ways to do it.
   - Too much social chitchat.

When you Communicate with a Thinker:

Begin with the beginning and present your message or question so it's easy for them to understand. Present facts—and substantiate them with additional facts. Speak calmly and precisely.

Avoid:
- Jumping to conclusions
- Waffling
- Leaving out details

When you Communicate with a Feeler:

Begin by recognizing them and asking a personal question. Show them you care or are interested in them. Create a friendly space. Allow time so they feel safe and understood. Speak as a friend and show that there is time for reflection and questions.

Avoid:
- Interrupting and do not force
- Confusing with abstract explanations
- Hunting for concrete knowledge or details

When you Communicate with a Changer:

Be open to new opportunities and give them space to look for new possibilities. Speak with tempo changes and listen for solutions. Match expectations and communicate a strong "why" so they understand your vision.

Avoid:
- Getting stuck on one possible solution.
- Getting bogged down in trivial details
- Focusing on personal gain or benefits

32

UNDERSTANDING YOUR INNER BALANCE

Most people are strongest in two personality types, meaning two sets of personality traits shine through in their competencies. The personality type that is most dominant for you will determine which of the characteristics you rely on when you're under pressure and out of balance. The Doer typically becomes dominant, the Thinker tries to control, the Feeler becomes insecure, and the Changer becomes an anarchist. The second personality type will support your primary trait, and for many people, that is enough. They don't bother stretching themselves to understand where other people are coming from or why they have a different take on a matter. When we discover our own balance, we can begin to see what is happening inside of us but also begin to work with our balance to become more complete as a human.

When we access the various competencies in the four personality types, we can more easily put ourselves in others' shoes and use the most appropriate competencies in a given situation. A person can gain access to nearly 100% of all the competencies in the four personality types, but it's very rare. Suppose you work extensively on your personal development. In that case, you will be able to get really far in terms of getting in touch with all your qualities and being able to draw on what is most appropriate in most situations. That means you can easily draw upon the most significant strategy in a given situation. You can also see and understand other people's perspectives and make them feel seen and understood. It will create fewer conflicts with other people and inside yourself. When you expand your abilities in the different personality type, it doesn't take anything away from the others. You simply expand your knowledge and ability to adapt and understand others.

Since we have practiced our first and second personality types for many years, they're easy and nearly free for us to use, which is why we prefer them. Stretching to understand another type or meeting other people's needs might be hard for us and cost energy, so we don't. Changing your priority personality type is possible, but people rarely do it. It can be that you use another type at work for many years and get really good at using these qualities. But when you get a new job, you will likely fall back into your old strategy unless the job requires the new skills.

Here are the combinations you can have for your first and second types. Be aware of how they can strengthen each other but also shut abilities from the other down. The first and second types can be nearly equal for some people, but there can be a bigger gap between them for others. See for yourself how they work inside of you and learn how you use the qualities from each one.

The example here can also be the other way around, depending on your balance. (Thinker-Doer, Feeler-Doer etc.)

If you are a **Doer** and **Thinker**, you may experience an inner conflict. Part of you wants to forge ahead, but another part holds you back, insisting that things need thorough examination first. If you become unbalanced, you may come across as very tough and dominating. When listening to both qualities, you will think before you act.

If you are a **Doer** and **Feeler**, you will have the desire and drive to accomplish great things but might be challenged by concerns about whether you're taking up too much space or if you're good enough. Your Feeler nature will prompt you to reflect but can also make you unsure about yourself or your abilities. Consequently, you might hold yourself back and appear weak. When both are in balance, you will have great empathy and impact.

If you are a **Doer** and **Changer**, there is no doubt that you will make things happen, but perhaps there is also a risk of being impatient or making too many changes too fast. Your Changer will hold the vision, and the Doer will push with more ideas and action. The best way to maintain balance is to practice the Thinker and Feeler strategies. If you keep using your Doer and Changer, settling down or keeping a job for an extended period will be hard. You can become restless and devise many excuses for not holding onto a project or a relationship.

If you're a **Thinker** and a **Feeler**, you may experience an inner conflict—part of you wants clarity and structure, while another part desires to delve into emotions. When you're aware of both aspects within yourself, it can be a strength. If your competencies are imbalanced, you may find that emotions take over in situations where you don't want them to, and you will then try to control your emotions. If this happens often, you will unconsciously try to shut down your emotions to control them. But if you do that, you also lose connection to your resources and will feel that something is missing or become sad. In a work environment with many Thinkers, it's sometimes tempting to shut off the Feeler side to be more like the others and feel that you belong. Doing so also means you shut down the finest qualities that define you, and you will slowly lose yourself. When you're in balance, you are very versatile in the workplace. You'll work seriously in-depth with things, maintaining a high level of professionalism while also displaying empathy and possessing the ability to communicate effectively.

If you're a **Thinker** and a **Changer**, you may excel in research and translating your ideas into innovative projects. You can handle complex analyses and see new opportunities and perspectives. Balancing the two strategies inside you can be a great resource. You will both be able to see possibilities and work out solutions to make them happen. You have to be aware that you can develop a feeling of superiority over others. If you don't practice your Feeler, you can become brutal if others don't live up to your expectations or deliver on the level you expect.

If you're a **Feeler** and a **Changer**, strong relations will be important to you. You will most likely have a great network and be popular, too. It will be easy for you to make new friends. Your focus will be making a difference to people. With a combination of high empathy and the inner drive to make a force for good, you are likely to work in an NGO or do volunteer work. It can be hard for you that you are not able to save all the people who need your help. You have to be aware not to take on everybody else's problems and also learn to set boundaries so you don't lose yourself.

PART VIII

Embrace Life and all the Challenges
Build your Inner Rock

33

UNDERSTANDING YOURSELF AND OTHERS YIELDS THE BEST RESULTS

In any interaction with other people, understanding them is crucial. When we don't comprehend other people's ways of being and acting, we might perceive their behavior as annoying or downright burdensome. As soon as we understand that others possess qualities and resources that we need—perhaps enhancing the overall result—a natural respect for others will emerge.

It is the awareness of which parts of the personality profiles we are strong in and the associated competencies that create the greatest understanding of why we are the way we are and react the way we do. In the same way, we will also gain a greater understanding of how others are.

With knowledge of your own strengths and weaknesses, you can consciously navigate situations more effectively, thus avoiding unnecessary conflicts, both with yourself and others.

When I'm aware that my Changer and Doer are dominant in my way of thinking, behaving, and talking to others, I also know to be more patient when I'm with a Feeler and more into details when I'm with a Thinker. You can begin to practice recognizing other people's personality types today. When you go shopping, notice how the Doers get impatient queuing and will quickly change to a different checkout if they think it will be faster. Thinkers analyze the queue and determine which one is better to be in. They look at the number of groceries, the people's age, and the speed of the person behind the till. Feelers usually enjoy chatting with other people in line, and Changers are busy inventing new ways to get through the till faster. They all have different strategies in different situations. When you become familiar with the other strategies, you will discover that you use them unconsciously according to the situation or the person you talk to. The more you can be conscious about it, the easier it will be to get along in any situation. And you might already be using qualities from your third and fourth personality types in different situations.

The best way to proceed from here is to practice and be curious. If you go to a family get-together, look at the others and see if you can determine their personality types. Talk to your friends and family and find out which types they are. That will also make it easier for you in your everyday life.

Since both my boys are Thinkers and Feelers, I have to be patient when they share something with me. Sometimes, it takes forever before they get started. If I just went along with my strategy, I would say, "What is it you want to say? Speed up, buddy; I don't have all day." But knowing that they need time and safety to open up, I breathe, smile, and wait. Then, they begin to share about their lives.

Exercise:

If you are not sure of your inner balance, you can download our free personality test app on app store or goggle play.

 App Store   Google Play

Write down your balance
1.
2.
3.
4.

What are the qualities you recognize from yourself?
1.
2.
3.

What are your weaknesses that you need to work on from the types?
1.
2.
3.

How do you react when you are under pressure or are tired?
1.
2.
3.

What do you need to be aware of?

Which one of the personality types do you have the hardest time dealing with?

Write down the qualities that annoy you:

Are these qualities in balance or out of balance?

Ask yourself, how can I be better at accepting this quality?

Is it a quality I don't have access to myself?

Which personality do you wish to strengthen inside of you?

List the qualities and how you will practice:

For example:

- I wish to be more organized (Thinker).
- I will try to make a schedule for my day
- I will make a list of all my tasks in the morning and cross them off as I finish them
- I will make sure to prepare more for meetings
- I will make a meal plan every Sunday morning

34

DO YOU WANT TO BE READY FOR
CHANGE?

Being ready for change is basically about how you handle your emotions and your behavior when changes occur.

The first step is to recognize how you feel about change and at what level the change is happening (renewal, change, or transformation).

It can be helpful to be specific about which changes challenge you. What one person experiences as trivial might completely unsettle another. When you pinpoint your challenges, it becomes easier to handle those situations as they arise. For instance, if you find it difficult when an appointment is rescheduled or when minor things in everyday life change, observe how you react in these situations. Do you become angry, irritated, insecure, or resigned? Or do you shut off your emotions and become dismissive? Subsequently, consider what triggers your reactions. Is it the feeling of not being respected, a loss of control, or perhaps a sense of not being good enough?

A change can be experienced as a loss. A loss of domain, tasks, influence, friends, job, skills, family, or colleagues. Therefore, you need to determine precisely which changes trigger you and the associated emotions. Once you're aware of this, the next step is to examine how you react in these situations. You will most likely respond in the same way each time, as we tend to use and repeat the same strategies if we find that they work for us.

Once you've gained an overview of which changes you can easily handle and which are challenging, try writing them down. After each, describe how you react when facing these challenges. (See the exercise below.)

When you know your patterns of reaction and what underlies them, you slowly become familiar with your emotions in different situations. You can begin to embrace yourself and your way of reacting. Once you can see your pattern clearly, you are one step closer to having a choice of behavior. Sometimes, our reaction happens so fast that we don't think; we just react. This is where you begin to practice Pause—Reflect—Zoom out. The first few times, you might still respond instantly. But when you keep observing and being present, you will get closer to breathing before reacting—creating a pause and a buffer zone where you get to choose the best way to respond. You might stumble and have setbacks, but don't worry. We all do. This is not easy; it takes practice and persistence. The most important thing is that you no longer react unconsciously and automatically.

The better you know yourself and the areas where you are challenged, the easier it is to welcome changes calmly and with resilience.

Exercise:

Changes I enjoy:

Changes I don't like:

After each change, add how you react and what you will practice in the future.

- **New work tasks:** *I get overwhelmed. I will try to address them specifically.*
- **New colleagues:** *I may become uncertain about my own abilities and my role in the team. I will focus on my strengths.*
- **Sudden changes:** *I become uncertain and might come across as harsh. I will try to breathe and connect with my emotions.*
- **A doctor's appointment is moved:** *I get irritated but let my boundaries be crossed and respect the other too much, so I don't say anything. I will try to speak up and stand by my needs.*

Try writing down your own examples to become aware of which situations challenge you and where you may be overstepping your own boundaries.

35

LEARN FROM LIFE

When we begin to see life as one big learning opportunity, our approach to change and challenges also shifts. No one goes through life without any obstacles. I met a woman who told me she had the nicest parents; they were always loving and supportive. Whenever she needed anything, they helped her. She had never faced any challenges, and then she got her first job and discovered that her upbringing was far from what other people experienced. She told me that her parents did everything to help her but didn't teach her how to deal with challenges or hard times. She wasn't resilient. Sometimes, we can wish for our pain or challenge to disappear, but ask yourself: Is this unavoidable? If yes, stop complaining and focus on what you can take responsibility for and where you can make an impact. And as you do, be present. With all the information available to us all the time and all the things that can steal our focus, it is more important than ever to practice presence. The brain has a rule: Use it or lose it. And when you are easily distracted or busy with what other people are doing all the time, your brain gets used to it and slowly lets go of the ability to focus. Many young people have several devices open at the same time. They have a chat window, YouTube, and their study on different screens—all at once. They will say that it is not a problem. But they don't know how the brain shapes itself based on what we do and how we use it. When you look at screens briefly and shift your focus, the brain finds no need to hold on to the ability to focus or have a deep conversation.

The brain feels rewarded when something is interesting. It's like going to a casino and playing the one-armed bandit. You press the button and hope for a win. When you don't get it, you try again. Every time, you get a dopamine rush, the hormone that makes us happy. A small win produces little to no dopamine, whereas a huge win would give more. Now, you will chase the next win to get more rushes. It is exactly the same thing that happens when you keep checking your email or social media. You get dopamine rushes, hoping there is a "win"—Something interesting, someone who reaches out, or something that makes you feel good.

When we lose the ability to focus and have deep conversations, our dealings with change and challenges become superficial. Even if we become aware of this, we need to regain the ability in our brain before we can begin to go deeper.

The more we ride on the surface, the harder it will be to dive down and see what is needed and the real cause. Our approach to change and challenges will be more superficial, and our focus will be more on the symptom than the real reason. It will be easier to blame others than to look inside to find the real reason and learning.

One place where most people can begin to practice presence and focus is when watching TV. If you watch a series, do you check your phone for messages or jump on social media? If you are like most people, the answer is yes. If you are watching a movie with your kids, are you checking your emails and maybe even answering a few emails, too? If you are, you are sending your kids a signal that focus is unnecessary. Soon, they will also play a game on their phone and watch TV simultaneously.

It can seem harmless, but it can have significant consequences for your brain and your ability to deal with change and challenges in your life. Everything we do is connected in the brain, and it's far easier to break something down than to rebuild it.

Presence is powerful. With presence, we build strong connections with other people, see each other, and learn through every step of life —the good things as well as the challenging things.

36

BE YOUR OWN ROCK

Now you know how your brain works, your survival mechanisms, and your inner strategy, and you know about unconscious fear and how to deal with it.

You are ready to build your inner rock so you can stand strong, solid, and grounded in your life and values. To make the knowledge inside this book most valuable to you, you need to begin practicing it. Many people read a lot of self-help books, but nothing ever changes.

I don't want you to be one of them. I want you to take the necessary steps to be your own rock.

Start with something easy. (Remember, make it easy and attractive). That way, you build confidence that you can deal with the bigger steps and challenges that life offers you. You observe your survival strategy, your emotions, your urge to fall into old patterns, or use your personality type to deal with the challenge. Maybe you feel like complaining or giving up. Fair enough, but then you remind yourself to observe your thoughts and emotions. And you ask yourself: What can I do right now to take a step in the direction I want? Small steps are better than no movement. And many small steps will get you there slowly, just like the tale about the tortoise and the hare.

The reason most people fail is because they are not doing the work. It's hard to stay on the path and take responsibility every single day. One of the hardest things is to be persistent. To support yourself, make a plan so you know what to do when you are about to give up. What can you focus on or remind yourself about?

When taking the small steps, you will be more motivated. Your brain will be happy reaching goals and ready to keep going. When I give lectures, I tell the participants to choose where they want to begin and look at where they are right now. If you don't know where you are, how can you know where to go? What resources do you have? How much time? Support? Skills? Money? Be realistic. It's much better than failing and falling back into old patterns.

We can't do it all at once. Many of us want a quick fix, but that is an illusion. There is no such thing, and if anyone tries to sell it to you, don't waste your money or time. Pick something you want to practice. If you tell yourself that what you pick is too unambitious, don't listen. Go with what feels right. The MAPPED model can help you work through the change or challenge. It will provide you with the clarity and support you need.

Acceptance is key to success. Don't shut down or pretend that all is good. Don't fight what you cannot change. Don't rush what is not ripe. Accept. Shift focus to what you can do and what you already have achieved that works for you.

Life is one big learning experience, and the more we can look at a challenge, a change, or a difficult time as a time to learn, the wiser we will be and more prepared for the future. We don't know what is ahead of us, and the more grounded we are and the deeper our roots are, the easier it will be to deal with whatever comes our way.

If we lose someone close, it will be painful. Don't shut down or try to make the pain go away. Turn to it. Become friends with it. Learn from it and shift your focus to areas of life where you have influence instead of fighting what you cannot change. In that way, you will move through life as a wiser person and build your own rock with every step you take.

Enjoy your amazing journey of personal growth and awareness.

I BELIEVE IN YOU.

37

MAPPED

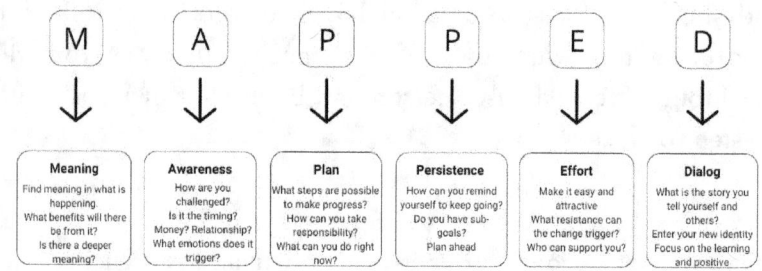

M	A	P	P	E	D
↓	↓	↓	↓	↓	↓
Meaning	**Awareness**	**Plan**	**Persistence**	**Effort**	**Dialog**
Find meaning in what is happening. What benefits will there be from it? Is there a deeper meaning?	How are you challenged? Is it the timing? Money? Relationship? What emotions does it trigger?	What steps are possible to make progress? How can you take responsibility? What can you do right now?	How can you remind yourself to keep going? Do you have sub-goals? Plan ahead	Make it easy and attractive What resistance can the change trigger? Who can support you?	What is the story you tell yourself and others? Enter your new identity Focus on the learning and positive

Whenever you face a change, challenge or difficult time, try to work through the MAPPED model to get clarity. It can support you in finding the meaning and learning, and the best way to deal with the situation. Sometimes it's good to go through the steps again after a week and see if new perspectives have arisen. In the workbook there are more questions and space to write too.

The change, challenge or difficult situation: (Describe it.)

MEANING:

- Find meaning in what is happening.
- What benefits will there be from it?
- Is there a deeper meaning?

AWARENESS:

- How are you challenged?
- Is it the timing? Money? Relationships?
- What emotions does it trigger?

PLAN:

- What steps are possible?
- How can you take responsibility?
- What can you do right now?

PERSISTENCE:

- How can you remind yourself to keep going?
- Do you have sub-goals?
- Plan ahead

EFFORT:

- Make it easy and attractive
- What resistance can the change trigger?
- Who can support you?

DIALOG:

- What is the story you tell yourself and others?
- Enter your new identity
- Focus on the learning and positives

Depending on the change situation or challenge , the questions in the model can vary a bit. You can use the model if you are facing a change, challenge or a difficult situation or if you are planning a change at work or in your private life.

RECOMMEND THE BOOK

I genuinely hope you enjoyed the book and that it will support you in being your own rock. I will be very grateful if you will write a review on Amazon, Goodreads, or Bookbub. It can be as simple as rating it or making a short comment. You are also welcome to write what you learned from the book, the most important takeaways or how you benefited from the book.

Scan me and review

I know you are reading a hard copy of the book and it's not easy just to click and review. But I hope you will grab you phone and scan the code. (Just open the camera on your phone and point it at the code. Then click the link that comes up.) In that way you can not only support me as an author, but help other people find the book and together we can make the word a better place with more consciousness.

Thank you,

Sagar

PS. I love nature, and if you find a great rock where you live, I would love to see it. Use the hashtag: #BeYourOwnRock. You can use the rock as a reminder to be true to yourself. Let's share great rocks!

ABOUT THE AUTHOR

Sagar Constantin is a bestselling Scandinavian author with more than eight books. She writes both fiction and non fiction that are both captivating but also highly inspirational.

She has a remarkable ability to make psychological issues easy to understand and comprehend. Through her reading, it is possible to grow inside and at the same time be highly entertained.

Sagar is also an international speaker and lecturer for businesses. Every year, she trains thousands of people in subjects like personal development, change management, EI, and leadership. Among her customers are LEGO, Fujitsu, Novo, The Danish Government, law firms and many more.

When she is not writing and teaching, she loves to spend time with her family and enjoys nature walks and sports. Sagar lives in Denmark but travels the world with her work.

GET IN TOUCH

To be the first to hear about new releases and bargains from Sagar Constantin sign up below.

(I promise not to share your email with anyone else, and I won't clutter your inbox.)

To sign up to receive the NewsLetter go here:
https://books.sagarconstantin.com/news

Follow Sagar Constantin on BookBub here: https://www.bookbub.com/authors/sagar-constantin

Connect with Sagar online:

https://www.facebook.com/SagarConstantinAuthor
https://www.instagram.com/sagar.constantin.author/
https://www.goodreads.com/sagarconstantin
https://www.linkedin.com/in/sagarconstantin/

Website: https://sagarconstantin.com
Mail to: info@sagarconstantin.com

Get the free downloads for the book here:
Sagarconstantin.com/byor

MORE BOOKS BY SAGAR CONSTANTIN

The In-Between series - All available as ebook, audio book, paperback and hardback.

Eva Monroe is returning from a three-week business trip, one in which she left her five-year-old son in the care of her estranged ex-husband when the plane that's taking her home crashes.

The accident leaves her in a coma, unresponsive to doctors' attention and the urgings of her little boy.

However, while Eva's body lies on the precipice of death, Eva's spirit has traveled to a place known as the In-Between - a world that is hovering in the clouds above our planet.

The In-Between is a temporary home for people where they must decide whether to return to their lives on Earth or move on to the next stage in their development.

It is a wondrous place, filled with spiritual aids and advanced technology. It is also a place where a person faces themselves fully for the first time.

When Eva arrives at the In-Between, she is utterly sure of her decision: she wants to return to her son.

Yet, she soon realizes that what she believes about herself and her place in the world isn't as straightforward as she'd always assumed.

And with this realization comes the understanding that her decision will be much harder to make than she ever would have guessed.

Thus, she is faced with the most challenging decision a parent can make.

Buy THE LIFE today to be drawn into a place that you never want to leave.

This is a riveting book! I wanted to stay up to finish it, but my eyes said no. It's the second book in the series and I highly recommend reading the first one before this book.

Angela returns to Earth to search for and find the last two members of a group called the Ring.

Together, the Ring can access crucial knowledge that the world desperately needs.

Each member has unconsciously carried a piece of this knowledge over thousands of years. By reconnecting the pieces, they will help turn mankind's negative, violent development on Earth into a positive, loving, and constructive progress.

If the Ring doesn't reunite now, it is doubtful that they will ever succeed.

Angela only has forty-two days to find the last two members and convince them to go to In-Between with her.

During her forty-two days on Earth, Angela's past, philosophy of life, and especially her sense of justice are challenged.

She must go beyond her limits, even when she sees her view of the world disintegrate.

The Ring is about standing firm and believing in something bigger than oneself.

It is about daring to live life to the fullest, looking death in the eye, letting go of the past, and having faith.

Through Angela's journey, readers will come to see the world as they have never seen it before.

Our world needs help. Our world needs hope. This amazing series of three books offer that hope. Read them, you won't regret it.

Very interesting book especially for the times we live in. The story line would have been easier to follow if I had read book 2, but it does explain enough to catch up. Life lessons taught - trust must be stronger than fear; love more important than hate; gratitude more than greed. With these there is HOPE.

If the Ring's mission is to succeed, Eva must travel back to Earth and try to stop Frank before he can reveal In-Between to the public.

Unfortunately, Frank has allied himself with a group of powerful people who want to gain power worldwide by spreading political and economic fear.

The task seems impossible, and as Eva is running out of opportunities, she sees no other way than to seek out a former friend. But for her to get help, she must break her promise to the Master.

Eva needs to work on her personal development to be a part of the Ring.

Only when all the members of the Ring have passed a test can they return to Earth with the knowledge and awareness that is crucial to the future of mankind.

Gabriel's condition worsens, and the Ring cannot be assembled without him.

Time is running out, and the question is, will Eva be ready on time?

Will she be able to let go of control and surrender to her vulnerability and her heart?

The In-Between series is available as paperback, ebook and audiobook.

www.ingramcontent.com/pod-product-compliance
Lightning Source LLC
Chambersburg PA
CBHW072136060526
44654CB00032B/427/J